BIOGRAPHIES
God at Their Sides

BIOGRAPHIES
God at Their Sides

Edited by
SISTER FRANCES HEEREY, S.C.H.

Illustrations by
GEORGE J. ANGELINI

The Regina Press
New York

1984
THE REGINA PRESS
7 Midland Avenue
Hicksville, N.Y. 11802

Book design and typography by Roth Advertising

ISBN: 0-88271-098-2

Printed in Belgium

Contents

Introduction

The appropriate action for any popular institution is to induct outstanding members into its special Hall of Fame. The sports world claims its most valuable players. The music world claims its favorite musicians. The movie industry claims its accomplished artists. The winners are chosen because of their outstanding talents and contributions to their respective institutions. They become role models for other devotees to emulate. The Catholic Church ordinarily celebrates its special Hall of Fame in the lives of its saints.

This book gives an account of the lives of outstanding contemporary Catholics. Most are people whose lives were marked by human struggles and by successful efforts to overcome difficulty through faith in themselves, in other people, and in God their Creator. Some fought for the basic human rights of others, the rights to life, food, shelter and education. Some used their literary, artistic, medical and communicative skills to bring God's message of love and salvation. Some dedicated their lives solely through priesthood or religious life.

The plain fact is that, in their own way, these individuals faced life with God at their sides. This is what has made them outstanding and role models for people everywhere.

My mother used to say, "The love of God is nearer than the door." She was right.

My father wrote the following portion of William Wadsworth Longfellow's poem "A Psalm of Life" in my Grade Eight graduation book:

> Lives of great men all remind us
> We can make our lives sublime,
> And, departing, leave behind us
> Footprints on the sands of time.

My father was a wise man.

May the lives of the people in this book provide inspiration for you to say "Yes" whenever Jesus calls you to follow Him.

Joseph Cardinal Bernardin

"I never took my religion for granted. I was really the only youngster on the block who was Catholic, so I grew up with a lot of people who became close friends but, for the most part, were not Catholic. Yet, I respected them because they respected me. I think I became much more sensitive to people, much more understanding."

These words were said in a newspaper interview given by Joseph Cardinal Bernardin, Archbishop of Chicago. The Cardinal humbly spoke of his life from early family days to his taking over the largest diocese in the United States. That means that Cardinal Bernardin has more Catholic people living in his Church territory than in any other Church territory in the country.

Joseph Louis Bernardin was born in Columbia, South Carolina on April 2, 1928. His father was from Northern Italy and was a stonecutter in the quarries in South Carolina. He died in 1934. Joseph's mother kept the family together by working outside their home. This gave Joseph and his young sister Maria the responsibilities of household chores and preparing meals. When Joseph was old enough, he also worked as a fruit and vegetable vendor. The money he earned helped out with school supplies for himself and Maria.

Joseph said that he had become a sensitive and

understanding person when he was very young. It was almost natural for him to seek a service career. He thought of becoming a medical doctor so he enrolled for one year as a medical student in the University of South Carolina. While studying to be a doctor he realized that the Lord was calling him to become a priest. To serve people as a Catholic priest became Joseph's one desire.

Joseph studied for the priesthood and was ordained in 1952. His first assignments were vocation director and secretary to a bishop. His Italian heritage, which he cherished most dearly, had left him with a warm and loving nature. Everybody was drawn to the gentle man who showed them a simple faith and deep spirituality.

When he was made Auxiliary Bishop of Atlanta in 1966, Joseph Bernardin was the youngest bishop in the United States. His talents soon brought him to the National Conference of Catholic Bishops. In 1974, he became president of that organization. Consequently, he became an advisor to the Pope.

In 1972, at the age of 44, Joseph Bernardin became the Archbishop of Cincinnati, Ohio. He loved the people of Cincinnati and they loved him. Imagine how sad they were one day when the Archbishop told them he had to leave.

In 1982, Pope John Paul II reassigned Joseph to lead the people of the Archdiocese of Chicago. The Chicago Archdiocese received him with great joy. When he first met with all the priests in that great Archdiocese, Cardinal Bernardin said to them, "I am Joseph your brother." He threw kisses at all the children who lined the streets to meet him. He cared much for all the people, especially the poor, and said he would work with everyone to solve the problems which affected their daily living. On February 2, 1983, Archbishop Bernardin was elevated to the College of Cardinals in Rome.

In the early 1980's, Cardinal Bernardin became chairman of a special committee of bishops who wrote a pastoral letter against nuclear war and for world peace. He even spoke to officials of the U.S. government and begged them to take world leadership in avoiding nuclear warfare. Many officials listened intently to this wonderful, peace-loving man.

A lot of success attained when one is young can sometimes tempt a person to look at nobody but himself. Luckily, one big lesson Joseph had learned was always to put the Lord first in his life.

Cardinal Bernardin always firmly believed that if you really respect people they will respond in a positive way. He has a great love of Jesus and Gospel value. He is a simple man of great faith. He is a great church leader.

Saint Frances Xavier Cabrini

Young Francesca's vivid imagination was at work again. She filled her tiny paper boat with flowers and sent it off to China with directions to feed the poor Chinese children. Her eyes, into which the blue Italian skies had spilled, sparkled with enthusiasm and desire. I must be a missionary also. Uncle Luigi's stories of faraway children had fed her imagination. Her dad's storehouse of maps placed the great land of China into the realms of possible travel one day.

Francesca Cabrini was the youngest of thirteen children. She was born on July 15, 1850 in Sant'Angelo Lombardy, Italy. She was tiny and frail from birth, and wanted to be a sister but was told her health would never stand the rigors of the life. However, she persevered and took her vows in 1877.

Soon after, Francesca started her own community of sisters called The Missionary Sisters of the Sacred Heart. Francesca had always wanted to go to China, but the Lord had other plans. He wanted her to come to the United States and care for the children of Italian immigrants. They needed food, clothing and shelter, just like the children of China.

It was Pope Leo XIII who gave directions to Francesca to go to America. After she pleaded,

"But Holy Father, I must go to China," Francesca heard him say, "You must go to America." After listening to the plight of the children in America, Francesca heard herself say, "Yes, Holy Father, I must go to America."

Heading a group of six sisters, Mother Cabrini, first Superior General of the Missionary Sisters of the Sacred Heart, began her first missionary voyage on a sailing vessel. How different from the paper boats she used to set on the lake at home. She got seasick!

Mother Cabrini arrived in New York on March 31, 1889. There was no one to meet this courageous group of women when they arrived. They had to spend their first day in a strange land in a roach-infested room. To make matters worse, the little group was told that they really were not needed and to go back to Italy.

At last, after her lifelong dream of becoming a missionary had finally come true, indifference, hostility and opposition met her head-on. The needs of the Italian children were great and Mother Cabrini had always given priority to the needs of children. In vigorous language and with an heroic sense of justice, she announced that she would stay in America! Besides, hadn't the Holy Father sent her to America?

Mother Cabrini set about the monumental task of rounding up the small children that were homeless beggars in the great city of New York. She and other sisters became like beggars as they went from door to store to tavern to bank, asking for donations for the children. How quickly they learned the English language! Orphanages were opened in the city. In 1890, with the help of the Jesuits, they moved up along the Hudson River on a big estate, called West Park. Fresh air, trees, grass and space were now free for the young boys and girls to enjoy.

Soon other cities sent for the sisters to take care of their children. Even Latin American countries heard of Mother Cabrini. The sisters opened schools for children who spoke Spanish and Portuguese.

Mother Cabrini liked to write letters to the sisters. One account tells of the time she was on a mule train. The driver, whom she called Joseph, needed a leader to jump a wide crevasse so they could continue their journey. No one wanted to jump first. Mother Cabrini prayed to St. Joseph, obeyed the leader Joseph, closed her eyes and jumped. She really was scared, but did not want anyone to think that a sister who believed in the protection of the Sacred Heart of Jesus could ever be afraid.

When Mother Cabrini saw the need for hospitals, she approached a bank manager. She politely told him how much money was needed to build a hospital. The banker smiled politely back. He said, "Yes, I see. There is much money needed to build a hospital. How do you intend to get it?" Mother Cabrini simply said, "You have so much. You can build the hospital." The banker was so charmed by Mother Cabrini's bold love of the poor that he gathered together other bankers and they built Columbus Hospital in New York.

Mother Cabrini had great insight into a social system that reeked of gross injustice. She sought with great determination to change the structures that prevented the poor from getting their fair share of food, clothing and shelter. She fought prejudice all along the way of her journeys as a missionary. It was her prayer, personal love of the Sacred Heart of Jesus and her simple faith, that made Mother Cabrini a true inspiration for thousands of young women to become Missionaries of the Sacred Heart.

As her life began, so it ended. On December 22, 1917, Mother Cabrini was helping prepare the children's bags of Christmas candy. Feeling tired, she went to her room to rest. Several hours later the sisters found her dead in her chair. It was as if she had said, "I've given my children food, clothing and shelter. I must go, peacefully, to the Lord."

Mother Cabrini was canonized a saint in 1946, and her feast day is celebrated on November 13th in the United States. She is the first American citizen to be so honored.

Cesar Chavez

Cesar Chavez was born on March 31, 1927, near Yuma, Arizona. He stands 5′ 6″ tall, and weighs about 165 pounds. His lank, black hair is covered with a straw hat. He has dark skin and flat cheekbones above which shine liquid Indian eyes. Small lips are tight under a bow-shaped nose. His whole face speaks of seriousness of purpose. However, a light radiates from his eyes when his wife Helen and their eight children hug him after his long day at work. Who is this man who attended thirty schools in California before he became a Grade Seven dropout? He is Cesar Chavez, the leader of the Mexican-American migrant workers.

Migrant workers are people who travel between orchards and farms, wherever the picking season calls them. The Mexican-American migrant workers have a long history of oppression. Cesar Chavez believes in the power of nonviolence in dealing with their oppressors. He once said, "Nonviolence can only be used by those whose cause is strong. It is very hard and man's self-control is very weak. I am not completely nonviolent yet, and I know it. That is why I fast."

Cesar had lived and worked in immigrant farm labor camps in California and Arizona. He understood the many problems that the Mexican-American migrant workers had. Chavez had an extraordinary dream. His dream was to right the wrongs his people suffered. Poorly paid workers, children as well as women and men, worked long gruelling hours picking grapes in the hot sun. Some workers stayed in open-air factories where the temperature hit 115°. Some people suffered heat prostration, and infectious diseases ran rampant. There were no medical facilities. Under those conditions most Mexican-American migrant workers died very young.

In 1952, Cesar joined the Community Service Organization. This organization was concerned with the plight of the Mexican-American migrant workers of the Southwest. Cesar eventually became general director of the Community Service Organization but became disenchanted. His dream was to establish a farm worker's union.

"What can I do to help my people be rid of these injustices?" Chavez asked himself. One answer lay in talking to the managers and owners of the farms and orchards. However, Chavez realized that he must first talk to the workers. Chavez's personality was such that he could make people listen. He helped the workers understand that they could bring about needed changes if they spoke about their sufferings. A core group of workers met with management and they expressed their grievances. People's work loads became lighter. They received better wages and their housing conditions improved a little.

However, Cesar had to accept the times when injustices were not corrected. He had to pray every day for patience, and it was not easy for him

to be patient. Cesar resigned from the CSO in 1962, and founded the National Farm Workers Association with his own life savings of $1,200.00. Through a home study course he learned how to become a fine bookkeeper. He kept honest accounts of the workers' wages and they trusted him. In 1966, the National Farm Workers Association merged with the Agricultural Organizing Committee to form the United Farm Workers Organizing Committee.

After the formation of the UFWOC, Chavez led a small group of California farm workers on a long walk to Sacramento, the state capital. Some Catholic priests joined the laborers. This was a daring deed. They wanted the government of this rapidly growing and wealthy state to know how poor some of its people really were. George Meany, head of the AFL-CIO said, "We are with you and we are going to stay with you until you have a real union." Chavez was happy. He said that a thinking union is fashionable today, but the labor movement, for all its faults, is one of the few institutions in this country that he could see even trying to reach down to the worker.

The injustices continued to crop up. In 1968, Cesar called for an international boycott of California domestic grapes. He knew that the owners of the farms, orchards and vineyards would have to suffer financially before they heard the cry of the poor. People all over the world joined in the boycott and management had to listen. In 1970, contracts were signed and conditions began to improve. These contracts officially recognized the

UFWOC as the union of the migrant workers.

God always raises up prophets when His people suffer unjustly. The world began to realize that Cesar Chavez is a prophet amongst the Mexican-American migrant workers. Because of one man's dream, dependence on God and love of the poor, seven million Mexican-American migrant workers have had a sense of dignity and pride restored to them.

Terence Cardinal Cooke

Whenever Terence Cardinal Cooke spoke of his father, he smiled his broad generous smile. He would say that his father, a chauffeur and tile-layer, taught him his most important lesson in life: "Whatever you do, do it with your heart."

"Heart" probably best describes Terence Cooke. He was born on March 1, 1921. As a young boy growing up in the Bronx, Terry was known as one who cared for others. He did it all in a quiet way. He did his school work well, played the violin, traded stories with his brother Joey and teased his sister Catherine. Family chores—such as running errands, raking leaves, tidying his room and drying the dishes—were done with generosity of heart.

Like many young boys who feel the Lord might be calling them to become priests, Terry went to Cathedral Prep High School in Manhattan. He was an average student. He studied at St. Joseph Seminary and was ordained a priest in 1945. Father Terence considered his priesthood his greatest treasure.

After working in a parish and a home for children, Father Terence studied for a master's degree in social work. He then taught at Fordham University for a while, and later took care of the housing and food needs of the young men at the Seminary where he had studied.

When Father Terence was named as secretary to Cardinal Spellman, Archbishop of New York, he accepted the job remembering his father's words, "Do it with your heart." He did such a good job that he succeeded Cardinal Spellman as Archbishop of New York in 1968. On April 28, 1969, Archbishop Cooke was elevated to the College of Cardinals by Pope Paul VI.

What were some of the activities that the new Cardinal became involved in? Remaining true to form, Cardinal Cooke entered into the lives of his friends, most particularly the other priests. He became a great leader in respecting human life, especially the struggle to keep babies from being aborted before they had a chance to be born. He was named as head of the Military Ordinariate which coordinates chaplain services to men and women in the Armed Forces and spent every Christmas after he became Cardinal in areas overseas where the forces of men and women were stationed.

Cardinal Cooke headed bishops' committees, ecumenical committees, hospital and educational committees. He supported the sisters and brothers who worked for the people in schools, hospitals or orphanages, institutes for the blind and deaf, day care centers, homes for the aged and in centers for unwed mothers. He helped Father Bruce Ritter establish Covenant House and Under 21. Cardinal Cooke served the homeless their meals on Thanksgiving Day and was a prince who walked with worldly princes and princesses and leaders of states. He laughed heartily at comedians who entertained decently and served as advisor to Pope Paul VI and Pope John Paul II on American Church affairs. He visited with his brother and sister and their children. The children all over the great Archdiocese of New York knew him as "Our Cardinal." When he was ill for several weeks, thousands of children wrote him get-well letters. What a magnificent heart he had!

It was the year 1977, when the much-loved Superintendent of Schools of New York Archdiocese, Monsignor James Feeney, died very suddenly. Cardinal Cooke honored Monsignor Feeney and his family by celebrating the funeral at St. Patrick's Cathedral. He gave his heart to the bereaved family and friends. A few weeks afterwards, a young, little-known woman worker in the chancery died. Cardinal Cooke visited the sorrowing family and celebrated the life and death of their loved one, in much the same manner as with the Feeney family.

When Tommy John, the famous New York Yankee baseball player, and his wife, were distraught over their young son who was in a coma, Cardinal Cooke visited the hospital. He prayed with the family and told them their baby boy would get better. The John family will never forget the moment their baby boy opened his eyes.

When Cardinal Cooke died on October 6, 1983, thousands of people of all religions and races flocked to his beloved St. Patrick's Cathedral in New York. They wanted to praise God for the marvelous graces given to a man who spent his life in the service of the Lord as a priest. "I couldn't think of a more joyful, more adventurous way to lead my life than to be a priest," Cardinal Cooke once told the young people at St. Patrick's Cathedral.

One can easily see why God chose Terence Cooke, son of Michael Cooke and Margaret Gannon, to be a priest, bishop and cardinal in the Church. Joy comes from the heart. All that Terence Cooke did he did joyfully, from his heart.

Dorothy Day

On the occasion of Dorothy Day's 80th birthday, Frank Sheed gave the homily at the Mass. He said, "Back in the early 30's, when Dorothy was trying to select a name for the houses she was founding, she didn't call them houses of charity because that is the coldest word in the English language. She didn't call them houses of love because that has to be the sloppiest word. No, she called them Houses of Hospitality. Now that is a word that hasn't been damaged yet."

Dorothy Day was born on November 8, 1897, in the shadow of the Brooklyn Bridge. She was the third of five children born to Grace and John Day. Dorothy's father was a sports writer who wanted his children to have a classical education. Mr. Day had made a wise decision. Dorothy and her brother Donald became excellent writers.

When Dorothy was six years old, John Day moved his family to San Francisco where they experienced the earthquake of 1906. Dorothy later remarked that it was at that time that she first saw people helping people in need. It left a lasting impression on her.

When the family moved to Chicago, they lived in a poor apartment over a store. Dorothy did not like living in poverty. When the family moved to better housing, Dorothy was relieved. However,

she did not lose her interest in the poor. When she was a high school student, she listened to people talk about the plight of the poor. However, they did not seem either able or desirous of really helping poor people in a practical way.

In 1916, Dorothy's career as a writer began. She got a job with a socialist paper, *Call*. As a reporter she wrote about the rights of workers and injustices that they suffered.

In 1925, Dorothy married Forster Batterham. Two years later they had a baby girl named Tamar Teresa. Tamar means "little palm tree." Beholding her newborn child, Dorothy knew there had to be a maker of all creation's beauty. Her baby stirred up some deep questions in Dorothy's life, about its goals, meaning and its source. She thought deeply about God. On December 28, 1927, Dorothy was baptized and became a Catholic.

In 1929, a terrible stock market crash occurred leaving horrible hunger, unemployment, homeless people and breadlines in its wake. It was at this time that Peter Maurin entered Dorothy's life. Peter was a worker and a dreamer. In his talks with Dorothy he painted pictures of people in need. He told Dorothy to start a newspaper to help rich people think clearly about the issues of poverty.

In 1933, Dorothy Day helped found the Catholic Worker Movement, and started a newspaper called the *Catholic Worker*. She took a great risk because she had no money available to run a publishing business. The first issue of the *Catholic Worker* was hand distributed. Dorothy mailed copies to other editors around the United States.

Dorothy Day spoke the truth about justice in her newspaper. She knew it was a mandate of the Gospel of Jesus. "We must speak the truth in justice," she wrote. Soon Dorothy was led to do the truth in justice. The poor began to knock on her door. She fed, clothed and housed homeless men. She restored to them a sense of dignity and pride. Dorothy made only one rule in her first House of Hospitality: Be what you expect the other fellow to be.

Dorothy opened many Hospitality Houses in cities around the country. She wrote, "Things are going ahead with the greatest difficulty. It is like moving mountains. We are surrounded with troubles. But for all the suffering I thank God."

Dorothy was a realist. She said that the poor were not always easy to get along with. She believed that the love of God demanded a special love of the poor.

Dorothy wasn't a person who prayed a lot. However, when the Lord showed Himself to her in the poor of New York City, she opened her eyes and her heart and made her home in Him. Every day she went to the nearby Catholic Church and received Jesus in Holy Communion. Dorothy died on November 29, 1980.

At her death, the New York Times and Commonweal magazine called Dorothy Day the most influential person in the history of American Catholicism. Can you see why someone once called Dorothy Day the Guardian Angel of the Unangelic?

Damien De Veuster

In the year 1888, an English gentlemen named Edward Clifford visited Molokai, one of the Hawaiian Islands. He stated that he expected to find the place scarcely less dreadful than hell itself. To his surprise he found lovely landscapes and cheerful people.

Everyone familiar with the history of the famed island of Molokai knows that it was once a paradise island. Polynesian people had settled on it about eight centuries after the birth of Jesus. They lived in peace and happiness, fished, grew abundant crops and picked berries and fruits. This wonderful way of life was hampered almost ten centuries later when Captain Cook and British seamen sailed into Hawaiian waters, visited the islands, and unfortunately left behind diseases which ravaged the happy families. In a short time only 50,000 people were left out of a once healthy population of 300,000.

One disease which decimated the population was leprosy. People's skin and bones wasted away. The victims became very depressed and despaired of any hope for cure. Oftentimes families had to be broken apart so that those without the contagious disease would not be infected. The people with leprosy were sent to a section of the island called Kalawao. Kalawao was surrounded by high cliffs,

which were covered with green vegetation. Waterfalls cascaded over the cliffs onto the peninsula floor. It was a beautiful land. However, the people were too ill to enjoy it. Sometimes the air became so damp that the sick people had to huddle together to keep warm. They truly were a suffering people. It was to this section of Molokai that Father Damien De Veuster sailed in 1873.

The son of Belgian farmers, Damien was born in 1840. He was ordained to the priesthood as a member of the Fathers of the Sacred Hearts, a missionary order responsible for Catholicism in the Hawaiian Islands.

Father Damien probably was very frightened when the boat which had taken him to Molokai pulled away from the shore leaving him all alone. Anxious eyes watched the priest as he made himself a shelter under a tree. His table was a large rock. When Damien finished his house, he sat back to enjoy a pipe. Puzzled, some people cautiously walked up to Father Damien. He greeted them warmly, "Hello, my brothers and sisters, I have come to make my home with you."

To gain the confidence of the people Damien immediately began to work with them, showing them a reverence for life that inspired them. They regained a sense of personal pride as they joined him in building proper homes, roads and a dock. They farmed and raised livestock. Convinced that music has healing effects on the soul and mind, Damien encouraged the people to make musical instruments. Often, in the cool of the evening, groups would gather together for a sing-song. They knew they were the little people that God loved so much. They grew strong in this love.

Damien knew it was important for Hawaiian government leaders to help bring proper medical supplies, doctors and nurses to the island. Damien spent many months convincing, not only the government, but his own religious congregation, that the people on Molokai had suffered great injustices. When the people showed signs of self-improvement, assistance flowed into Molokai. Damien's reputation spread throughout the world. His personal suffering increased when jealous people accused him of being a popularity seeker! Damien had succeeded where others had failed. In 1881, he received the Hawaiian Order of Knight Commander of the Royal Order of Kalakoua from Princess Liliuokalani.

One morning as Father Damien was showering, he did not feel the hot water which had splashed on his body. He knew immediately that he had contracted the disease of leprosy. He truly was a brother in the leper colony of Molokai. He joyfully prepared for his death amidst the people to whom he had brought the justice of a loving God, but would live for another five years. He died on April 15, 1889.

Where did Father Damien De Veuster get his courage to do the things he did? Brothers, sisters, priests, and lay people in the Church today can tell you. They help people in parishes, neighborhoods, cities, hospitals, drug clinics, universities, schools, anywhere in the world where there is a need. They call upon the Lord in prayer every day and He gives them courage to do things they never dreamed of doing.

Jean Donovan

Hands in pockets, Michael Donovan looked at me over his glasses. "People ask me if I ever think of my sister Jean as a saint. No, I don't think of her as a saint. I think of her as my little sister."

For several years I had pondered the meaning of Jean Donovan's life and death. Like thousands of other people who watched a 1980 TV report in horror, I saw Jean's body dragged from a shallow grave in El Salvador. With her were three other slain missionaries, Sisters Maura Clark, Dorothy Kazel and Ita Ford. These four wonderful women were in love with the poor, suffering, beautiful people of El Salvador. For their kindness and care Jean, Maura, Dorothy and Ita were brutally murdered.

My fascination lay with Jean Donovan. She was born on April 10, 1953, in Westport, Connecticut. She had one brother, Michael, whom she idolized as her "big brother." Her parents, Ray and Pat, bright, active members in church and civic affairs, provided a comfortable home for their children.

Michael and Jean had countless opportunities for an excellent education and healthy recreation. Softball, basketball, swimming, bike-riding and horseback-riding were their sports. Jean sat a good saddle and spent many hours running with her horse, breathing in the excitement of the chase,

jumping and splashing through low sparkling river beds. Jean and Michael relished their moments together. Childhood days were happy days.

During college Jean's exuberance marked her as one who truly loved life. She graduated in 1975, and acquired degrees in economics and political science. Jean received her master's degree in business management and accounting from Case Western Reserve University in 1976. When she was offered an office job in Cleveland, she accepted it. Characteristically, she brought life to her place of work.

Jean was an active member in the Legion of Mary. The Legion is a society which offers a way of life and prayer to its members. Reflecting on her future life, Jean said, "I've come to the realization that I've got to do something for other people. There is something more I want to be."

She joined Kaleidoscope, a church-related group of young people. Amidst the fun and joy Jean found with the group, thoughts of helping others lurked in the back of her mind. She heard about Cleveland's diocesan mission in El Salvador. Jean knew she wanted to go there, and said, "I want to give some time to God's work. I've had a lot of privileges in my life. One of them may be the capacity to help others who don't have much."

In the fall of 1979, Jean attended the Maryknoll Lay Missionary Program in Ossining, New York. There she learned about the language, customs and traditions of the people of El Salvador. Jean arrived in El Salvador in 1980, and was met by a wonderful Ursuline Sister, Dorothy Kazel. Together they worked with the people. Jean did the practical chores of bookkeeping and taking care of nutritional needs. She fell in love with everyone, particularly the children. She led a youth choir, taught the young people about the beauty of their bodies, minds and souls. Most especially, they learned from Jean how much God loved them. The children grew more deeply in their faith each day that Jean was with them. They loved her dearly.

On March 24, 1980, Archbishop Romero was killed while he was saying Mass. This hateful act disturbed Jean. She was afraid but she would not leave El Salvador. She wrote, "I love life and I love living. Several times I have decided to leave. I almost could, except for the children, the poor bruised victims of adult lunacy."

Jean Donovan found her reason for staying in El Salvador. It was the little children. She consoled them when they lost their mothers and fathers, and she hugged them close when they were afraid. She sang with them when they played games. Jean loved and she was loved. In this she imitated Jesus who loved little children.

On December 2, 1980, Jean drove with Dorothy Kazel to the airport to meet two Maryknoll sisters, Maura Clark and Ita Ford. After they had left the airport in their jeep, Jean and the other missionaries were brutally murdered. The good people of El Salvador were shocked and saddened to lose these wonderful women. Like Jesus, the four missionaries had given up their lives for their friends.

Jean Donovan is considered a martyr and a saint by me and many other people. For Michael Donovan, this martyr is his "little sister."

Tom Dooley

If you need information for a social studies assignment on the people of Southeast Asia, you will do well to read Doctor Tom Dooley's books, *The Night They Burned the Mountain*, *Deliver Us from Evil* and *Edge of Tomorrow*. Dr. Dooley's stories of the Vietnamese and Laotian people tell of deep faith, love, gentleness and great bravery. While reading the books you will come to know the author whom Americans call their "Splendid American." Tom Dooley leaped over the honors and riches of the world to treat the medical and physical needs of people miles away from his home.

Where did young Doctor Tom receive courage to become an American hero? He gives personal insight in several places. One source is a quotation from Hippocrates' "The Precepts." Written 2300 years ago, the message contained an impelling challenge for Tom.

Sometimes give your services for nothing, calling to mind a previous benefaction or present satisfaction. For where there is love, there is also of the art. For some patients recover their health simply through their contentment with the goodness of a physician.

Another powerful force in Tom Dooley's life

was his daily praying of the "Our Father." He started that practice as a small boy and he never lost it.

Tom was born on January 17, 1927, in St. Louis, Missouri. The four Dooley children had an exceptionally happy home life. Mr. and Mrs. Dooley taught their children about God's love. They encouraged their children to be generous with their talents.

During World War II young Tom interrupted his studies at Notre Dame University to be a hospital corpsman. He graduated from Notre Dame in 1946, and received his medical degree from St. Louis University in 1953. He enlisted in the United States Navy as a medical officer and was immediately assigned to Vietnam. There he was given the responsibility to care for 600,000 Vietnamese refugees who had fled the Communist government in the northern part of their country. Miraculously, Dr. Dooley set up a tent city and established a medical clinic for the people. He especially loved the children who were so frightened but who got better quickly under the care of the friendly *bac sy my*, their American doctor. Tom Dooley wrote, "With my own eyes I had seen the enormous power of medical aid in all its Christlike simplicity." In 1955, he received the Legion of Merit from the U.S. Navy.

In May 1955, Doctor Dooley was very sad. He had to leave Vietnam. He firmly believed that medical aid, offered on a people-to-people basis, could do a lot to join the peoples of the East and West in true friendship. Prompted by this conviction he re-

signed from the Navy, entered Laos in 1956, and opened a clinic in a jungle area of that country. Each year 50% of the Laotian babies died. Dr. Dooley put together a traveling clinic, and used an old jeep to search out mothers and sick people who needed medical help. Dr. Dooley saw the people as "clots and clusters of the withered and wretched in Asia." Yet, he received much inspiration from them. He saw homeless refugees at Mass every morning at dawn, where they thanked God and asked no favors for themselves.

Doctor Dooley had the help of Notre Dame University recruits. After a long day's work in the hot jungle, the young unselfish men would join the doctor in praying the Family Rosary. Doctor Dooley wrote, "It is sometimes hard to see God when you are plunged into a brash materialism. It is easier in the jungle. Here we can know God a little better."

Doctor Dooley called upon the generosity of the American people for his noble cause. The response was outstanding and medical supplies poured into his camps. He proudly told the Laotians about the wonderful Americans who shared their hearts and wealth with them. In time Doctor Dooley established MEDICO. The Medical International Cooperation Organization provides health services in underdeveloped areas of the world. Doctor Dooley persuaded the famous Doctor Albert Schweitzer to be its patron.

Tom Dooley was said to have an appetite for a high quality of life. He said, "I believe that God has put us on this earth not merely to exist from day to day, but to use our time in the service of others." Until the Lord called him home on January 18, 1961, Tom Dooley lived what he believed. A citation which he received a year before he died reads,

The epic sings of arms and a hero,
the arms of mercy and compassion,
the hero of our Splendid American,
Doctor Tom Dooley.

This "Splendid American" was an inspiring model of an authentic medical doctor.

Dr. Lena Edwards

"*I* am going to be a doctor. I know it will be difficult for me. I'm a girl, I'm black, and I am a Catholic. These are wonderful challenges to me. I am only 12 years old but I know I can be what I want to be. And, I am going to be married and have a lot of children."

Lena Edwards was born in Washington, D.C., September 1900. Her mother, Marie Coakley Edwards, was the daughter of Gabriel Coakley, a gentleman who spent many hours collecting money for the first black Catholic Church in Washington. Black Catholics did not always find a welcome feeling when they went to Church to worship God. Lena's father was a dentist. Her parents' love and the example of her family spurred Lena on to do great things with her life.

Lena was successful in her studies at school. In 1924, she received her M.D. Soon afterwards she married a handsome young doctor, L. Keith Madison. Lena and her husband chose Jersey City to set up their practices. She worked at the Margaret Hague Maternity Hospital. Together she and Keith raised six children, four sons and two daughters, two of whom are doctors and one a priest.

Lena had a deep faith in God and a great love for St. Francis of Assisi. She also had a great love of people, especially her family. Former patients smile when they recall being in Lena's office and hearing her say, "Please excuse me one minute. I hear my baby crying."

God has different ways of calling people to Christian service. One way is by serving Him as a lay Franciscan. Lena centered her life in the Church as a lay follower of St. Francis. Despite a successful career and a growing family, Lena did not close her eyes to the cry of the poor. She thought, "Both Jesus and St. Francis had a preferential love for the poor. I want to be like them. What better way to show this love in action than by opening a clinic for poor expectant mothers." At the age of 54, she gave six years of volunteer time to the migrant laborers in Texas. Lena operated her maternity clinic and health care center for them, using her own money to do so.

Lean taught at Howard University in Washington, D.C. The United States Department of Labor appointed her lecturer on labor conditions, and she was made a life member of the Catholic Interracial Council of Washington, D.C. Even in her old age, Dr. Edwards has not retired from living a full Christian life. She still helps the poor, the elderly, the underprivileged.

Courage, determination, love of God and people, helped the twelve-year-old Lena reach her dreams of being a medical doctor, a married women, and a mother. How proud her family and friends are of Dr. Lena Edwards. Her country is so proud of her that they gave her the President's Medal of Freedom, the highest honor the U.S. can bestow on a civilian. How delighted Jesus and St. Francis must be with their friend and devoted follower!

Father Edward Joseph Flanagan

"Many hands make light work," Mrs. Flanagan sang merrily to her children as they busied themselves with the chores on their Irish farm. Young Edward Joseph loved these hours with his family. He watched his father train his young brood to respect all living things, the crops and animals, but most of all their family members. Edward was filled with pride and gratitude. His Dad would often bless himself as he praised the God of all living things. He would counsel in earnest, "Remember now, the love of God is nearer than the door."

Edward Joseph Flanagan was born in Roscommon, Ireland on July 13, 1886. He left Ireland in 1904 to study for the priesthood in America. He sorely missed his family, and tears would well in his eyes until he was in his late teens. After completing his studies at Mt. St. Mary's, Maryland, Dunwoodie, New York, Rome and Innsbruck, he was ordained in 1912.

From 1912 to 1917, Father Flanagan worked in parishes both in and around Omaha, Nebraska. Many families and individuals there were suffering from poverty due to unemployment. During this time, he received permission to open the Workingmen's Hotel, which was a shelter for down and out workers. He used his own little store of money and asked for donations from others.

Father Flanagan was deeply disturbed at the increasing number of vagrant boys who were coming to the shelter. He felt that a home, food and clean clothes were the best remedies for the terrible sickness which society had inflicted on these boys. He believed that plenty of chores would make the hours happy and profitable ones for the boys. Father Flanagan had a creed by which he lived. He believed in Jesus Christ, His Church and the power of prayer. He also believed that there is no such thing as a bad boy.

In 1917, he opened a Home for Homeless Boys. Two of the boys were newsboys and three were referred to him by the Omaha Juvenile Court. In 1918, Father Flanagan bought Overbrook Farm outside Omaha, and this is considered to be the beginning of Boys Town as we know it today. The number of boys increased daily and they came from all races, were all colors and professed all religions. The boys were received into Boys Town with love.

It wasn't always easy for Father Flanagan. Some boys had formed habits of lying, stealing, cheating and swearing. There were fights. There were tears. There were great triumphs when honesty and kindness became the code of many boys who had been the "number one bullies." What was Father Flanagan's secret? He knew Jesus' advice about forgiving seventy-times-seven times. The troubled boys who constantly repeated their patterns of bad behavior were forgiven and given chances to start over again.

Boys Town became a legal municipality in 1934. The boys took on the roles of mayor, lawmakers and judges. By the time that Spencer Tracy and Mickey Rooney made the movie *Boys Town* in 1938, Boys Town and Father Flanagan were known throughout the world.

As a result of this, he was asked by governments and private groups in the United States and abroad to consult on the problems and care of cast-off boys of every description and nationality. After World War II, at the request of U.S. officials, he traveled to Japan, Australia and throughout Europe to show those peoples what he had done and how he had done it. A trail of new Boys Towns followed his appearances.

Father Flanagan died on May 15, 1948, in Berlin, Germany.

In 1983, the first graduation class of girls took place in Boys Town. The presence of girls has changed the atmosphere of the place to a small degree, but the spirit of Father Flanagan lives on. His respect for life has spilled over into the lives of others who continue to operate a school of love, forgiveness, and encouragement. "The love of God is nearer than the door!"

Sister Irene Fugazy

"I gratefully accept this Eddy award on behalf of members of my news team. I wish to thank my parents, my communications moderator, Mr. Christopher Salvador, Sister Irene Fugazy and the staff of ITV for giving us opportunity to learn the television communications medium. Thank you." With these words a thirteen-year-old girl, holding high her Eddy trophy, stepped off the platform in Studio A. Popular members of television networks presented other awards to the eagerly awaiting contestants for their successful work in educational television communications. Excitement ran high. Sister Irene Fugazy, director of the Instructional Television Studio, smiled with satisfaction at the students' accomplishments in communications.

Irene Fugazy was born on October 3, 1918, in Greenwich Village, New York. Greenwich Village is a section of New York City where life is full. Many creative and artistic people live there. Irene and her brothers, Louis and Bill, grew happily under the great love of their parents. They had many challenges for education in the arts and business fields. Their home was filled with happy chatter as the family planned their next adventure.

Summer fun was found in horesback riding. The three children rode with their mother and father up in the Catskill Mountains. At the age of four Irene rode her own horse. Louis, Irene's older brother, was very athletic. Irene idolized Louis. She told herself that anything he could do she could also do. Louis drove a car at 16. Irene drove a car at 14.

Irene was intensely interested in dramatics. She acted in school plays in her parish drama club at St. Joseph Church. All the while she thought seriously about her future life. By the time she was in Grade 8, she had made up her mind to become a sister. She just knew deep within her being that was what she should do.

Irene's father objected strenuously to her decision. Life had so much to offer his bright and attractive daughter. Irene said, "No one can change my mind. It is a grace. If I give up the call to religious life, it will be giving up a grace." God had given Irene an unusual insight into the meaning of the word grace, which is understood as a "Gift from God," indeed a gift of God's own life. Irene honestly admitted she tried to forget about the gift, but it would not go away.

Devotion to the indwelling of God has been the source of Sister Irene's strength throughout her life. She was professed a Sister of Charity in 1936, and became a brilliant teacher. Her talent for dramatics helped her write plays. Her first play was on the life of Mother Elizabeth Seton.

The Lord blessed Irene with a marvelous sense of hospitality, graciousness and humor. These qualities suited her for public relations work. She was assigned as public relations director for Elizabeth Seton College in 1963. People grew to love and greatly respect her even disposition. Sister Irene seemed ever sensitive to the needs of people, whether they were Cardinals, university educators, big business people, ordinary teachers, parents or students.

In the late 1960's, Sister Irene was asked to direct the expanding educational television studio in Yonkers, New York. With a ready response to the challenge, Irene became Director of Instructional Television. She knew that the use of TV as a medium for education offers a myriad of new and exciting possibilities for learning. Communication skills include listening, reading, reporting, graphic arts, slides, photo essays, interviewing and eye witness reports.

Sister Irene has opened the ITV doors to various associations for educational purposes. Associations of doctors, lawyers, business people and educators have used the ITV facilities. Sister Irene wisely sees that the Gospel message can also be spread widely through the use of ITV. Many programs are broadcast on the Bible, the life of Jesus, prayer and evangelization. Some Sunday Scripture readings are done through the use of mime.

Under Sister Irene's direction, daring and wise planning, the largest United States Instructional Television Fixed Service signal (ITFS) was set up, covering an area of 4,714 square miles. Some celebrities who have helped Sister Irene in raising funds to support the system have been Bob Hope, Joe DiMaggio, Dorothy Hamill, Billy Martin and her own brother, Bill Fugazy.

One wonders how the mind and body of one small woman can hold so much talent and graciousness. Sister Irene will tell you herself that besides gaining much from her wonderful family and friends, she learned much about love and simplicity through studying the life of St. Elizabeth Ann Seton. God who dwells within her had never ceased to have an attentive audience in the heart of Sister Irene. It is from Him that she has learned the art of communication.

Helen Hayes

"It's because I was pigeon-toed, you know, that I am an actress at all," the renowned actress, Helen Hayes, told a reporter in a newspaper interview. She smiled the beautiful smile of an elderly woman who had spent her life doing good for others.

Helen Hayes was born October 10, 1900, in Washington, D.C. Her father, Frank Brown, was a wholesale butcher. Her mother, Catherine Hayes Brown, had a wonderful sense of drama. For hours she entertained her young daughter Helen, who responded with a spontaneous giggle. For Helen, it was a natural school for education in dramatics.

In order to straighten Helen's tiny feet, which had a tendency to point inward, Mrs. Brown sent Helen to ballet school. One evening when she performed in a children's recital, a talent scout was in the audience. He decided that the young Helen had a natural talent for acting and a quick intelligence to learn directions. Helen was not even five years old. "That was the beginning of my acting career," Helen later reminisced.

Mr. and Mrs. Brown sent young Helen to Catholic schools in Washington, D.C. and in New York when the family moved to that city. Helen had happy school days and thoroughly enjoyed dance and acting classes.

Eventually, Helen became an accomplished actress. Some popular movies and plays she acted in were: *Pollyanna, Penrod, Dear Brutus, The Ladies, We Moderns, Airport* and *Candleshoe.* In 1931, she won an Oscar for the movie *The Sin of Madelon Claudet.*

Whenever Helen Hayes talked about her many wonderful years of acting on stage and in the movies, she would become quietly reflective. She realized that God had given her the talent to act. Helen used the gift to entertain other people and always acted with sincerity. She was always a gracious lady and would not allow producers to give her parts that were loud, cheap, or immodest. Commenting on the sex that is shown in the movies and television today, Helen Hayes claimed that it has had a very bad effect on the real romance of the world. As a result of her high standards and Christian morals, Helen Hayes became known as the First Lady of the Theater. In 1955, a Broadway theater was renamed the Helen Hayes Theater.

Besides acting, Helen Hayes took time out to marry a playwright, Charles MacArthur. Despite their busy schedules and many travels, their marriage lasted until Charles' death thirty years later in 1956. Helen often remarked that their love grew stronger as the years went by. Her faith in God's love and her husband's love never grew weak.

Being a very generous and compassionate person, Helen devoted voluntary time to handicapped people. She especially loved working with children, who, she said, gave her more pleasure than all her stage and screen acting. A hospital in Haverstraw, New York, is named the Helen Hayes Hospital.

Helen Hayes published a book called *A Gathering of Hope*. It contains portions of poems, sayings, and writings of other people which had been sources of reflection to her. She found them so good she wanted to share them with others.

Helen Hayes has loved the Catholic Church all her life. She has loved God and His people, the Church. She prays every day, thanking God for His wondrous gifts to her. Mother Teresa said to Helen one day, "You do so much good." Can you see why Helen Hayes, Academy Award winner, has become a very special person in the twentieth century world?

Father Theodore M. Hesburgh

"Cheer! Cheer for old Notre Dame..." The college band struck opening chords. Thousands of football fans lucky enough to get tickets for the game sang the rousing words. The Fighting Irish ran proudly onto the field. College President Theodore M. Hesburgh smiled in triumph, but for another reason. Because his ten-point program related to televising collegiate football games had been adopted, American television viewers could, for the first time in history, watch the game in their homes. It was the year 1953.

Father Hesburgh had finished only one year as president of this major American university in 1953. The successful television project was the beginning of many notable events which he headed to raise the University of Notre Dame to its present status. Thousands of people point proudly to the famous Golden Dome and say, "I graduated from that Catholic college." They are lawyers, psychologists, computer experts, doctors, theologians, teachers, liturgists and peace and justice leaders. Father Hesburgh is equally proud of the graduates. He knows that hard work helped them achieve their goals. Father Ted boasts, too, of the wonderful faculty and supporters of Notre Dame's ideals. With Father Hesburgh's style of leadership, Notre Dame stands tall and proud.

Syracuse, a city in northern New York State, warmly welcomed its newest citizen on May 25, 1917. Theodore and Anne Marie Hesburgh could not have known the great things in store for their squealing baby, whom they had baptized Theodore Martin. God's gift of vocation was planted early in the boy's life. Determined to become someone special, the four-year-old Ted announced he would become a priest.

Ted was educated in Syracuse Catholic schools. In 1934, he enrolled at Notre Dame College in Indiana. Even though he loved football, his theology studies were more intriguing. After matriculation, young Ted entered the Seminary. On June 24, 1943, he was ordained a Holy Cross Father. For the next nine years Father Hesburgh continued studies, worked as chaplain for the Army and at the National Training School for Boys and a Washington reformatory. He became a teacher at Notre Dame University, and later on the Executive Vice-President. At the age of thirty-two, he became President of Notre Dame.

While a seminarian, Ted had given Father Patrick Peyton assistance in starting off the Family Rosary Crusade. He learned to call daily on God and Mary for help in all his work. Later, as Father Hesburgh, he wrote that he strongly believed that God needs people, particularly boys and girls, men and women, to bring Christ's saving message to the world. He saw Notre Dame as one place for that to happen.

During the 1960's, a period of unrest fell on university campuses. Young people violently pro-

tested seeming injustices. They caused extensive property damage. Father Hesburgh stood tall and challenged the would-be rioters at Notre Dame to look for rational solutions to social problems. Violence only causes pain and fosters violence. Even though his stand was not popular with everyone, Father Hesburgh kept Notre Dame University operating peacefully. Students who stayed benefited from Father Hesburgh's wisdom as well as their own efforts at learning.

More than three decades have passed since Father Hesburgh took office as President of Notre Dame University. During that time he has generously given his talents to the church, the country and the world. He has written thought-provoking theological materials. In 1964, he received the President's Medal of Freedom. Father Hesburgh was also a representative at sessions of the International Atomic Energy Commission.

Most important, Father Hesburgh has been a model for energetic college students who are grateful for their faith and God's love for everyone.

Grace Kelly

If what people have always said about the dreams of little girls is true, then Grace Kelly of Philadelphia had a once-upon-a-time-there-was-a-Princess Grace-dream. And like many young girls throughout history, Grace Kelly's dream came true. She did become a princess, to Prince Rainier of Monaco. Monaco is a tiny principality on the Mediterranean Coast.

Grace Kelly was born on November 12, 1929. John B. Kelly, Jr. and his sister Grace were a very close brother and sister. Brought up in a wealthy family, they had the opportunity for a good education and for training in sports and the arts. The Kellys had a wholesome respect for the things of God and His people. They learned their religion, worshiped God in the Catholic Church, and took care of those people less fortunate than themselves.

Young Grace specialized in dramatics and tried for Hollywood roles. Imagine the surprise and pride of the Kellys when Grace announced she had won a role in a film. Not only did Grace act well, she soon became famous for her extraordinary beauty, charm and goodness. In 1954, Grace won an Oscar for her role in *The Country Girl.*

When Prince Rainier of Monaco met Grace Kelly in person, he fell in love with her. The Prince asked her to marry him. To do so would mean giving up her career as an actress. Grace prayed very hard that she would make the right decision. She loved Prince Rainier so she chose to become his wife! On April 18, 1956, Grace Kelly became Princess Grace of Monaco. Her acting career in Hollywood ended. Grace grew more popular as the celebrated, well-beloved Princess Grace.

Soon God sent three children to the Grimaldis, Caroline, Albert and Stephanie. As a full-time mother Grace spent long hours with her children. Princess Grace knew that her children, because they were members of a royal family, would have to attend ceremonies that promised to be long and formal. She wanted them to have happy memories of childhood play and laughter and taught them how to swim, to ski, to cook and to clean. Most of all, she taught them what it means to love.

Besides being a full-time parent, Princess Grace had to attend state functions. She presided over many charities with great social charm, kindness and graciousness. Some of her greatest acts of charity became known when people talked about what the Princess had done for them or members of their family.

On September 14, 1982, the Grimaldi and Kelly families, the people of Monaco, the members of the acting profession, indeed, the whole world was shocked to learn of the sudden death of their Princess Grace. You see, Grace Kelly had become everyone's princess. They loved her for who she was: wife, mother, sister, daughter, friend, actress, entertainer, benefactress, princess. They praised

her for what she stood for: truth, honesty, loyalty, faith, love of God, love of people and belief in a life hereafter. Princess Grace was an outstanding contemporary Catholic.

Rose Kennedy

When Rose Kennedy called her children to dinner, she made certain that eleven places were set in readiness for them. She and her husband Joseph would spend many hours with the lively brood as they chattered during an enjoyable family meal.

Rose Fitzgerald Kennedy was born on July 22, 1890. She was the daughter of Mary Hasson and John Fitzgerald. John Fitzgerald, also known as "Honey Fitz," was a prominent politician and the Mayor of Boston from 1905 to 1914.

Rose Fitzgerald married Joseph P. Kennedy on October 7, 1914. During their marriage, Joseph P. Kennedy would become one of the wealthiest and most influential men in America, as well as the Ambassador to England. Rose knew she would need assistance in her role of mother, not only from her husband Joe, but from spiritual sources as well. Each morning after the children were fed, washed, dressed, and sent off to school or play, Rose went to Mass and Communion in the parish church. She strongly believed that faith was a living gift from God. It would help in making value choices and be a source of comfort when trouble came. She prayed that her faith would grow stronger each day so that she could help her husband and her children be happy and successful human beings.

Rose Kennedy nurtured her children well. Besides providing them with examples of kindness and love she saw that each child received and valued a good education. Every day the house would hum with the sound of children reciting their lessons. Sports were considered very important for healthy bodies and minds. The nine Kennedys were active in many competitive sports. With so many children, Rose boasted of having two home teams to play touch-football in her own backyard!

Because Rose Kennedy was an outstanding member of the Church and local community, she received an award from Pope Pius XII in 1951. She was made a Papal Countess.

Both Rose and Joe taught their children that they must give something back to society. They were very fortunate and had been given many opportunities. Because of their parents' insistence, the Kennedy children made it a point to help those in society who could not help themselves. Rose Kennedy told her children that she would rather be known as a mother who raised a famous son or daughter than a person who was known for a work of art.

Rose raised five daughters. They are Rosemary, Eunice, Patricia, Jean and Kathleen. You will probably know the names of Rose's sons. They are John F. Kennedy, U.S. Senator and President of the United States; Robert F. Kennedy, Attorney-General of the United States and U.S. Senator; Edward M. Kennedy, U.S. Senator; and Joseph P. Kennedy Jr., World War II hero.

Despite an abundance of material possessions, Rose has suffered through many personal tragedies, the foremost of those being the deaths of Joseph Jr. and Kathleen in airplane crashes and John and Robert by assassination. One of life's most painful experiences for a parent is to bury a child. Rose has lived to see four of her children die tragically.

God has tested Rose throughout her life, and she has remained a pillar of strength. This strength comes from her deep faith and tremendous love of God. She truly loves God, her family and her friends. Mass and prayer, an integral part of her daily life, are also sources of strength for Rose Fitzgerald Kennedy, a beautiful and loving mother, and an outstanding American.

Father Maximilian Kolbe

"The Blessed Mother offered me two crowns, white and red. I told her I wanted both: white, signifying that I wanted to persevere in purity; the red, so that I can be a martyr."

The person who wrote these words as a young boy was Maximilian Kolbe. He was the man who voluntarily took the place of another prisoner in the horrible prison camp at Auschwitz and was tortured and killed there. He died on August 14, 1941. Father Maximilian Kolbe, a Catholic priest, was canonized a saint by Pope John Paul II on October 10, 1982. On that day he received the two crowns he had asked for, the martyr's crown and that of the chaste man.

Raymond Kolbe was born on January 7, 1894, in Zdunska Wola, Poland. His parents, Maryanne and Julius, had their son baptized Raymond in the Church of Our Lady of the Assumption. When he was 13 years old, Raymond entered the Franciscan Seminary, and took the name Brother Maximilian. Raymond felt a strong desire to spread love for God and His Mother by preaching and writing about them. It was during his years in the seminary that Maximilian became ill with tuberculosis. This disease would plague him for the rest of his life.

During his seminary days, he organized a

group of Franciscans called The Knights of Mary Immaculate. After ordination in 1918, he became a teacher. In 1922, Father Maximilian followed his heart's desire to write by establishing a magazine called *The Knights of the Immaculate*. With the help of friends, he bought his own printing press. Other brothers helped the young priest with writing, printing and circulation.

In 1927, Prince Drucki-Lubecki donated a large tract of land outside Warsaw to Father Kolbe and his followers. This would come to be known as the City of the Immaculate or Niepokalanow. In less than twenty years over seven hundred men joined Maximilian in his work. It was like a miracle! The men built a novitiate, friary, hospital, fire department and radio station! The friars worked together to spread the love of God and Mary. They even sent Father Maximilian to Japan to do the same missionary work. Before long over 20 Japanese men had entered the Franciscan Seminary. Father Maximilian told the men that the reason he was always so happy was that he knew one day he would go to heaven!

In 1936, Father Kolbe returned to Poland. He fearlessly spoke out against Adolph Hitler and the Nazis, who would invade and occupy Poland in 1939. The friary at Niepokalanow became a refuge for displaced persons. About two thousand Jewish people were cared for by Father Kolbe and the Franciscan brothers.

In February of 1941, he was placed in jail by the Nazis and eventually sent to a concentration camp named Auschwitz. Even though he and the

other prisoners worked hard and were mistreated, Father Kolbe knew that the Nazis could never harm his soul. He said, "Hatred is not creative. Our sorrow is necessary so that those who live after us will be happy." Like Jesus, Father Kolbe was kind to those who made him suffer.

One day he saw a young Polish man being sentenced to death. Father Kolbe said to the jailer, "Take me. I have no wife or children. I'm old and not fit for anything." He was tortured and starved over a three-week period before finally being put to death by an injection of carbolic acid. The prisoners and jailers marvelled at how brave Father Kolbe had been.

This is what Segmond Gorson of Wilmington, Delaware, remembers about Father Kolbe. Mr. Gorson's parents were murdered in Auschwitz camp.

> Kolbe found me. He was like an angel to me holding me, wiping away my tears. He gave me back my faith. He dispensed love and nothing but love... He gave away so much of his meager rations to others that it is a miracle he could live. Not only did I love Max Kolbe in Auschwitz where he befriended me, I will love him till the last breath of my life.

Father Maximilian Kolbe, a Knight of Mary, founded the largest Franciscan Friary in the world. He was an expert in the art of communication. He helped the suffering during World War II and died a martyr. On August 14th, the Catholic Church will remember to praise God for Father Maximilian Kolbe, modern saint.

Vince Lombardi

In 1959, Vince Lombardi became the head coach of the Green Bay Packers. They were an uninspired team, and had won a total of four games in the previous two seasons. However, Vince did not let this discourage him. He was both a master psychologist and strategist, and constantly pushed his young team to its physical and mental limits. Lombardi told his players that "Winning isn't everything. It's the only thing." He was a disciplinarian who commanded the respect of his team, and convinced the Packers that they could become NFL champions.

His creative strategies and unlimited confidence in his men did make winners out of the Packers. He had moved players into unexpected positions, and helped them to adjust to his brand of football. By demanding that plays be correctly executed with no "ifs, ands, or buts," the Green Bay Packers would become one of the greatest teams, if not the greatest, in the history of the NFL. Green Bay, Wisconsin would become known as Title Town, U.S.A.

Vince inherited his strong sense of command from his father. Henri Lombardi emigrated from Italy and owned a wholesale meat business in Sheepshead Bay, Brooklyn. His wife, Matilda Izzo, was a warm, loving woman who gave her children love and taught them respect for all living things and a sense of the presence of God. Mr. Lombardi was a hard worker who saw to it that his children studied, worked, prayed and grew into proud citizens of the United States. With his brothers Harold and Joseph and his sisters Madeline and Clare, young Vincent learned a healthy self-discipline.

Vincent Thomas Lombardi was born in Brooklyn, New York on June 11, 1913. Because of his strict and religious upbringing, he desired to be a priest as a youngster. After two years at Cathedral Prep, he realized he no longer had a vocation and enrolled at St. Francis Prep. He was excellent both as student and athlete, and starred as a fullback on the football team.

Dennis J. Carey, an industrialist, brother of former New York Governor Hugh L. Carey and a classmate of Vince at St. Francis Prep, said "Vince was very quiet, extremely studious and a tremendous football player. However, none of us ever expected the great things that followed."

In 1934, Vince enrolled at Fordham University and majored in business. He was a guard on the nationally ranked football team and a member of the famous "Seven Blocks of Granite."

From 1939 to 1947, Vince was the football coach at St. Cecelia High School in Englewood, New Jersey. In 1949, he became an assistant to Red Blaik at West Point. Working under Blaik would be a significant decision for Vince. It was under this great coach that Lombardi would find his niche as both an offensive genius and a strong leader of young men.

Vince joined the New York Giants as an offensive coach in 1954. In the previous season they had a record of 3-9, and both a terrible offense and defense. Under his direction, the offense was revitalized and the Giants won the NFL Championship in 1956, their first in sixteen years.

When Vince accepted the position of head coach of the Packers in 1959, he and his wife Marie moved their family to Green Bay, Wisconsin. By 1961, the Packers would win the first of an unprecedented five NFL Championships. During his years in Green Bay, the Packers would become one of the greatest teams in NFL history, and Lombardi one of the NFL's greatest coaches.

Marie Lombardi believed that football would eventually break Vince's heart. Vince believed in total dedication and wanted to build strong bodies and strong characters. However, the younger players began to lose some of their incentive as owners began to give in to their demands. This upset Vince greatly—how prophetic Marie's words were!

Vince Lombardi died of cancer in 1970. People from all walks of life and all corners of the world admired his abilities and success. Vince was a man who remained true to his ideals of hard work, excellence, and love of God. He would become a hero and legend in American society. "Never pray for victory," he once said. "Pray for the will of God."

Clare Booth Luce

Clare Booth Luce, Ambassador to Italy, magazine writer, Broadway actress and film star, congresswoman and convert to Catholicism, once remarked that she had a love affair with brains. This is an intriguing statement from an accomplished woman who has been honored with several honorary degrees but who has never graduated from high school.

Clare was born on April 10, 1903, in New York City. When she and her brother David were small children, their parents divorced. Their mother Anna, an actress, had difficulty making enough money to support her children. Times were hard and Clare's mother wanted her children to be successful in life despite their poverty. She challenged them to be the best in whatever they set out to do.

Clare attended the Castle School in Tarrytown, a small village up along the Hudson River. The girls said that she was the brightest, most artistic student, and prettiest girl in their class. Clare liked to write doggerel verses. These comic jingles gave merriment to her classmates. A few teachers raised their eyebrows but smiled as they recognized Clare's clever intelligence.

Clare had movie screen tests taken in Fort Lee, New Jersey. She got an acting part in a picture called *The Heart of a Waif*, and later had parts in

Broadway plays and enjoyed a short acting career.

Clare fell in love and married George Brokaw in 1923. They had a lovely daughter, Annie. There was great sadness when George died in a swimming pool. Clare and Annie became good friends who enjoyed funny things that happened at school. Clare and Annie vacationed together and shared sight-seeing trips. Then another serious accident occurred that took the life of Annie. She died in a car crash when she was on her way home for a college vacation. Clare took Annie's death very hard.

Clare's talent for writing got her jobs with the popular magazines, *Vogue* and *Vanity Fair*, but her success lay with photography. In 1935, she married Henry Luce. She and her new husband, who was the owner of Time Inc. and *Life* magazine, reported world news through life-like photographs of people in action. Clare's work brought her into contact with many important people. Her ability to relate well made her a popular figure in society. She was elected a congresswoman in 1943, and worked in Washington at that post until 1952. In 1953, she accepted the post as Ambassador to Italy. It was the first time that a woman had ever been appointed an ambassador. Among her famous friends Clare lists Madame Chiang Kai-shek, Frank Sheed, President Eisenhower, Winston Churchill, Nelson Rockefeller, Mark Clark, William Buckley and Lord Beaverbrook.

Clare had deep questions about life. She certainly had her share of sorrow. Her loved ones had all died and she was left alone. Women of her time had to struggle to succeed in business. She sought answers to her questions by visiting a priest. Satisfied that the Church could help her, Clare became a convert in 1946. Monsignor Fulton Sheen, a prominent preacher and teacher, baptized her and gave her the sacraments of Holy Eucharist, Penance and Confirmation.

Clare chose St. Therese of Lisieux as her model. Therese, known as the Little Flower, had a "hidden way" of loving God and people. She recognized that it is the little things in life that are important, and kept hidden what she had to suffer. This quiet love and gratitude to God for all good things in life seemed to be for Clare the best way of Christian living. She daily received Jesus in Holy Communion.

If you should ever get chance to go to Mepkin, South Carolina, take it. On a 7,000 acre estate you will find a Trappist monastery which once was Clare Booth Luce's home. There, in the quiet of the woods and farmland, you will understand better the spirit of Clare Booth Luce, outstanding woman, editor, fashion plate, playwright, author and Catholic.

Sister Maria Goretti Mannix

The special school supervisor was coming today. Children, teachers and the principal stood in eager anticipation outside St. Aloysius School awaiting Sister Maria Goretti Mannix. As she walked up the Manhattan street, Sister Maria recalled that it wasn't too many years before when she was principal of St. Aloysius School. She quietly thanked God for her teachers and everyone else who helped her become a success in life.

Sister Maria Goretti, named after a young twentieth-century Italian saint, was born in 1929, to Eulalie Matthias and Kasper B. Mannix. Eulalie came from Trinidad as a baby. She conscientiously pursued education and became the first black woman to graduate from the Columbia University School of Pharmacy. She eventually bought a pharmacy at 119th Street and 7th Avenue. Eulalie Mannix ran the New York Pharmacy for twenty-five years. Sister Maria Goretti's dad was from Antigua. He studied hard, too, and became a successful master electrician.

Maria had a happy time with her brother, Kasper, and their baby sister, Rachel, as they played and did their lessons above their mother's pharmacy. Love, laughter and liveliness reigned in their home. Father and Mother Mannix were always present to hear lessons, patch up little quarrels, and teach their children right from wrong.

Young Maria made friends with some Catholic school children in the neighborhood. She sometimes walked with them to church services. She asked her parents if she could attend the Catholic school, where, she said, she would not get into any more fights. Quietly, Maria's mother studied to become a Catholic. She, Maria and Kasper were baptized in August of 1939. In September, the children entered St. Thomas the Apostle School.

After graduating from Cathedral Girls High School in New York City, Maria worked for a year. In 1950, Maria surprised everyone when she announced that she planned to enter the congregation of sisters called the Franciscan Handmaids of the Most Pure Heart of Mary! Even though her father did not wholeheartedly like the idea, Maria did become a Catholic sister. Because of his great warm love, Mr. Mannix eventually glowed with pride upon his daughter Maria's success.

Being a sister takes a lot of energy. Sister Maria trained as a teacher. She taught at St. Thomas Mission School in Wilmington, North Carolina. Many of the children were Baptists. They were very poor. Sister Maria taught the little children how to read, write and do arithmetic. Sister Maria watched the parents build a community school with their own hands. Another surprise came when Sister Maria was brought back to Harlem to teach for two years at St. Aloysius School. Then she taught for five years at her former school, Cathedral High. Imagine the happiness of the children when Sister Maria returned as the principal at St. Aloysius.

Like her mother and father, Sister Maria was destined for success. In 1976, Sister Maria became Superintendent of all the Catholic schools in Manhattan. What a privilege for the children! Sister Maria provided principals and teachers with educational programs that helped them deal with children of many races, religions and capabilities. She became a great leader in local, state and national associations.

In 1982, Sister Maria was called by her religious congregation to become Superior General of the Franciscan Handmaids of Mary. Sister Maria said in a newspaper interview, "I believe the Franciscan Handmaidens are something for people to look up to; in part, because we are the only sisters with a motherhouse in the heart of Harlem. We give witness to the Church, to Christ, and we are living witnesses to the fact of living a Christ life."

The black community and the educational community have been proud of Sister Maria Goretti Mannix. They see a sister devoted to children and parents. They see an educator who believes in Catholic education. They see a woman who lovingly has given her life and heart to Jesus as a Catholic religious sister. Sister Maria Goretti has worked hard all her life. The beautiful thing is that she has done it all cheerfully and graciously.

George Meany

"A plumber with brains? All plumbers have brains, George. Make sure, George, that you use yours." With these words George Meany was challenged by his dad to take the intelligence that God had given him and use it to its fullest advantage.

As a young boy George Meany used to sit quietly on the floor in the parlor where his dad and a group of men gathered. They would talk about the local politics at Union 11. George's dad was president of Union 11. It was at those sessions that young George started his love affair with ordinary people who labored as plumbers, carpenters, electricians, tradesmen and skilled craftsmen. This love affair eventually brought George Meany to be recognized as the greatest labor leader in the United States.

George Meany, familiarly known as "Brother," was born on 125th Street in Harlem on August 16, 1894. When he was five, his parents moved the family to St. Luke's Parish in the Bronx. There, with his nine brothers and sisters, Brother did all things young, energetic people found exciting. He rode the trolleys during the summer and watched the neighborhood blacksmith shoe horses. He played stick ball, football and ring-a-leavio. His greatest love, however, was baseball and catcher was his favorite position. Despite his love for the game, George stopped playing baseball when he was 22.

In 1919, he married Eugenia McMahon, an embroiderer at the ILGWU. His father had died a few years before, and George became responsible for his wife and children, as well as his mother and the younger members of the Meany family. He made a pact with himself that he would devote all his nonworking hours to them exclusively. George's fine dancing style, his humor at parties, and his devotion to Church and personal prayer, soon became his trademarks as a "family man."

The world best remembers George Meany for his prowess as a business agent and labor leader. He often said that the standard of work which people performed was awfully important. He inspected the work at construction sites. If it was of poor quality, he would order, "Tear it out!" He would arrive early at a job, ride the elevator or hoist to the top, walk down with the workers, talking with them, trying to find out if their working conditions were safe, if their hours were good, if their wages were just and their compensations fair. He had a tremendous facility for taking complex problems and reducing them to simple terms. Meany could be trusted! He admitted, "I work hard and I am very lucky."

George Meany is credited with bringing industry and labor together to talk about common problems. He was a forceful speaker and used common sense in his business dealings. He began his career as a journeyman plumber in 1915, and became involved in the labor movement. In 1922, he was elected to the staff of Plumbers Union Local 463. He was elected president of the New York State Federation of Labor in 1934, and secretary-treasurer of the American Federation of Labor in 1939. George became president of the American Federation of Labor in 1952, and was instrumental in its merger with another powerful organization called the Committee for Industrial Organization. This new organization was known as AFL-CIO, and George Meany served as its president from 1955 to 1979. George became a powerful spokesman for labor, and took a strong stand against Communism and corruption within organized labor.

The AFL-CIO was founded to care for people who had no power to speak for themselves. George frequently had to meet with big politicians and the Presidents of the United States. They respected George, who presented pictures of the real needs of the American worker. He brought great benefits to men and women who do the building, repairing, and maintaining of the towns, cities and villages that make up the United States of America.

George Meany died on January 10, 1980.

What does all this mean for us? It shows how important it is to recognize that honest work, done well, makes us great in the eyes of God and of people who are important to us.

Thomas Merton

If someone had asked Thomas Merton if he were a mystic, he would have replied that if his seeing a good ball game, enjoying an intriguing mystery movie, taking moments to pray, breaking bread with a friend, or breathing fresh air were some indications of what a mystic was supposed to be all about, he would have said quite readily, "Yes, you could say that I am a mystic." Thomas Merton was a mystic, a writer, a religious seeker and a monk.

The son of Owen Merton and Ruth Jenkins, Thomas Merton was born in Prades, France on January 31, 1915. He was tenderly cared for by his mother who delighted in his baby antics, aliveness and merriment with things of nature. His father Owen was born in New Zealand. Thomas' paternal grandmother had been born in Cardiff, Wales and had settled in New Zealand. When his grandmother visited the Merton family in Flushing, New York, she made a profound impression on young Tom. He wrote, "The general impression she left was one of admiration and awe and love ....There was nothing effusive and overwhelming about her affection...She taught me the Lord's Prayer, which even though I did not say it for many years, I did not forget it."

Thomas' mother died when he was six years

old, leaving him free to travel with his father who was an artist. They even lived in Bermuda for a while where Thomas attended an all-white school. Sometimes he was in school; sometimes he was not. He traveled so much that he did not know that most other children did not have a similar life.

When Thomas was 10 years old, he settled in France with his dad. He developed a warm love for France. He loved the silence in the valleys and countryside. At one of the schools, however, he experienced a great hostility. A summer spent with his private family restored a peacefulness that balanced the unhappy days spent at the Lycee.

Thomas later lived in England with his Aunt Maud, a charming lady. By this time his father had become ill and died of a brain tumor. Young Tom was left without parents in a strange country. While he was in England he attended Cambridge University and met some of the best writers, actors and painters in the world! At this time he discovered William Blake, an English poet.

He later attended Columbia University in New York, where he wrote a thesis on William Blake. Thomas led a different life catching the fever of expectation while taking on different jobs, visiting exciting places in Europe and the United States. One day he discovered that with all the interesting things that he was doing he was basically unhappy. He could write. He could paint. He worked as a baker. He worked at a sideshow. He hung around with a rowdy college crowd. During his search for the meaning of happiness Thomas was led to the Lord. Tom said that William Blake led him in a round-about way to the only true Church, and to the One Living God, through His Son Jesus Christ. It was during this period of time that comparisons can be drawn between Thomas' life and the life of St. Augustine.

Thomas converted to Catholicism in 1938. In 1941, he decided to give himself to the Lord as a Trappist Monk and entered the Abbey of Gethsemani, Kentucky. Thomas wrote about his desire to be a priest in these words: "I cannot say what caused it. . . . It was not a thing of passion or of fancy. It was a strong and sweet and deep and insistent attraction that suddenly made itself felt, but not as a movement of appetite toward any sensible mood. It was a new and profound and clear sense that this was what I really ought to do."

Thomas wrote his famous autobiography, *The Seven Story Mountain*, in 1948. He was ordained in 1949, and began to write about the spiritual life. His writings became popular. He was asked to take on the spiritual direction of other men. He helped them to see what he had discovered, namely that transformation was a key to his own spirituality. It was a quest for Christ. The monks knew cold and heat, hunger and its satisfaction, joy and weariness of labor. They became acutely aware of birds, flowers, trees, sky, stars and all of creation. They became aware that they were finding and loving the God of all creation.

As a final crowning of his discovery that he was really human, and founded and redeemed by Christ, Thomas said, "Thank God, thank God; that I am like other men, that I am only a man among others. It is a glorious destination to be a member of the human race."

Thomas Merton died on December 10, 1968, in Bangkok, Thailand, where he was attending a conference. An electric fan fell into the tub and he was electrocuted. The world was shocked. It was as if they had lost a voice that said, "We are weak, we are not saints, we are proud, self-centered little guys, who want to belong to God." And Thomas had assured them all that it was the story of humanity. It was that humanity that Jesus took upon Himself and made rich and good and holy. And it is for this reason that so many people who read Thomas Merton's autobiographical works feel that they can put their own name at the end of them.

Bishop Emerson Moore

"Mom? Dad? How are you? I've a bit of news for you. Your son E.J. is going to be ordained a bishop." With that news, Emerson Moore, a Harlem-born priest, hugged the two dearest people in his life. His mother and dad were an inspiration for his good living, a support to his conversion to Catholicism, his support to ordination to priesthood. Now they could smile a broader smile because their family, friends, and the whole black community in Harlem, would celebrate their son's ordination to bishop!

Emerson Moore was born in Harlem, N.Y., on May 16, 1938. When people first meet him, their immediate impression is that he is a man for others. There is a contagious excitement about his life and about his work for the cause of peace for a suppressed people. When he was made Vicar of Harlem, Bishop Moore said that his main thrust would be to make black Catholics feel more at home in the Catholic Church.

One of "E.J.'s" school chums at PS 40 observed that Emerson was a very studious, special person: "When he reached his teen years, it became evident that Emerson was following a course slightly different from the rest of us." E.J. was tagging along with a group of children, led by Mrs. Rivera, to St. Augustine Church in the Bronx. Each Monday night Mrs. Rivera attended the Novena devotions. In 1953, at the age of 11, E.J. was baptized a Catholic with his two sisters, Dorothy and Patricia. Mrs. Rivera, a neighbor, was largely responsible for his conversion to Catholicism. What had made the Catholic Church a place of special interest for E.J.? He liked the ceremonies and the rituals and the discipline.

The boys at Cardinal Hayes High School in the Bronx had great respect for Emerson. He had a certain manner of friendliness, yet he held a reserve that made them realize he was going to be someone special someday.

When he was a student at St. Joseph Seminary at Dunwoodie, Emerson spent much time with children. He invited them to the seminary grounds for outdoor fun. It didn't matter whether they were white, brown, yellow, or black. They were children and he loved them all. One great moment in his life at the seminary was the baptism of his parents into the Catholic faith.

After he was ordained, in 1964, Emerson was sent to work in a parish in Harlem. He became active in community affairs because he saw a great need for proper housing for many people who lived below the poverty level. He saw a great need for attention to the education of the young people. He and the other priests eagerly stayed with the children in the school and in the playgrounds.

One of the highlights of Bishop Moore's life was the visit of Pope John Paul II to the people of Harlem. The thrill of meeting the Pope was great. The message the Bishop received was sent to all

black communities in the United States. The message was, "The Lord knows no color." In 1982, Emerson Moore was appointed Auxiliary Bishop of New York.

Bishop Moore has a dream. It is that lay people be actively involved in the church. He said once, "I'd like to see developed a strong sense of community, fellowship, togetherness—real unity among people, black, brown, white, whatever. And I'd like us all to become more prayerful, make a commitment to the Lord in a real way, and work together to build up the kingdom of God."

Every bishop has a coat of arms that he designs at his ordination. Bishop Moore's sign says: ONE LORD, ONE FAITH, ONE BAPTISM.

Flannery O'Connor

The smoky train chugged into the small station in rural Connecticut. Stepping onto the platform box, a young woman was greeted by her two friends, Sally and Robert Fitzgerald. "Flannery!" they cried. "Over here. It's so good to have you come."

That is the kind of attitude that everyone had who knew Flannery O'Connor, novelist. It was always good to be with her. Why? Because she was humorous, yet she was serious about the right things in life, like family, friendship, work, and most importantly, God and Church.

Flannery was born in Savannah, Georgia, on March 25, 1925. She loved her mother and father very much and they loved her. Flannery wasn't a sporty type, and enjoyed going to parochial school. In college she used to draw cartoons, and entertained everyone with her wit and candor. Eventually she became editor for the college literary magazine, *The Corinthian*. In 1945, she received her degree from Georgia State College for Women.

For a while Flannery lived at Yaddo, in Saratoga Springs, New York. While there she met a famous professor and author named Robert Lowell, one of America's finest teachers. He recognized that Flannery had great talent to become a

famous author. She disciplined herself every day for that to happen.

Discipline is a writer's must. Flannery herself said, "The fact is, if you don't sit there every day, the day it would come well, you won't be sitting there. . . I write only two hours every day because that is all the energy I have; but I don't let anything interfere with those two hours."

In 1950, at the beginning of an active career as a writer, she contracted lupus. Her dad had died of lupus when Flannery was just 16 years old. Courageously, Flannery went in and out of the hospital for nine months. She eventually lost her power to walk. She needed much rest and quiet. Almost miraculously, she began to fulfill Robert Lowell's prophecy about becoming a good writer. During her career, she would become friends with Thomas Merton.

She gained a power to write novels. Flannery used to spend a lot of time thinking about people and life. She seemed to sense the weaknesses of human beings and she wrote about the very human things that people do. Because she had a great sense of humor, she portrayed her characters in various funny stages of life. Although she wrote in a comic strain, Flannery's novels were really serious stories about life and characters who were very weak. Some titles of her novels appear strange. In senior year of high school and in college courses, students read *Wise Blood* and *The Violent Bear It Away*. In those novels readers discover Flannery's unique understanding of the redemptive nature of suffering. Flannery beautifully understood Jesus' words, "I've come not to save the just but sinners." Flannery really believed and loved this Jesus very much.

Flannery received Holy Communion every day. She celebrated Jesus because she celebrated life. One time she was at a dinner party when some guests facetiously questioned what Catholics believed in, especially the Holy Eucharist. Flannery listened quietly. When everyone had finished speaking, Flannery firmly told them that her whole life and faith were based on Jesus in the Holy Eucharist. It was her honesty and simplicity which made her a strong, witnessing Catholic. Flannery died on August 3, 1964, after a long struggle with lupus.

Can you see why Flannery O'Connor was fun to be with? She was bright and witty. She wasn't wishy-washy at all. She knew what she believed and she was not afraid to speak the truth when it was time to speak up.

Archbishop John J. O'Connor

Three thousand pairs of attentive eyes were raised upward to the high greystone pulpit in St. Patrick's Cathedral. Enraptured teenagers listened to the new Archbishop's spirited homily.

"Antarctica provided me with the most wonderful experience in life. It was 40° below zero and summertime in the lovely blue waters which appeared between two massive ice columns. On my right was a natural ice tunnel filled with rainbow-colored stalagmites and stalactites. It was a dazzling breath-taking moment when God's magnificence flooded my soul. How I praised God for the beauty of His creation!

"Outside a large flock of curious penguins awaited me. Their leader waddled over, stood in front of me, eyed me, shook its head from side to side, and returned to its mates. The penguin's chagrin upon close inspection of me was truly a humbling experience. I took my turn and examined the funny tuxedoed birds and discovered to my amazement that no two birds looked exactly alike. A little patch of yellow on the face of one, a clipped ear on another, the height of birds here where no one ever sees them? I was captured by the mystery of God's reasons for giving life to whom and what, wherever and whenever He wishes. I was more convinced than ever of the mystery and sacredness of life.

"Now I look out at your wonderful faces. No two are alike. You are so sacred. Your life is part of God's mystery, part of His plan in creation. How sacred you are. How much God loves each of you. How much I love you. How much I need you to love me.

"You are the Church. I am not going to tell you what the Church will do for you. I am asking you what you will do for everyone in the Church, the unborn, the handicapped, the elderly, the poor, the needy."

A hushed silence. Breaking it was a thunderous applause. Three thousand teenagers accepted the challenge. "Right on!" they shouted at the charismatic Church leader who brought them warmth and cheer. They knew with certainty that they were loved because they were made in the image and likeness of God.

Even before Archbishop John J. O'Connor arrived in New York, newspapers and magazines were filled with stories of this intriguing man. He was a priest, bishop, teacher, author, lecturer and Rear Admiral. He had several educational degrees. He wrote books. He flew planes. He was an all-around athlete.

John J. O'Connor was born on January 15, 1920, in Philadelphia, Pennsylvania, to Dorothy and Thomas O'Connor. Learning from them gentleness and industry, John worked huckstering for a farmer, delivering Western Union telegrams and repairing bicycles. He was intrigued by his father's skill as a gold-leaf craftsman, and gained from him a deep sense of justice concerning the

rights of laborers. Because of his native intelligence and wit, he excelled in studies, drama and sports.

John experienced stirrings for a missionary life. The Holy Ghost Fathers and Maryknoll Fathers appealed to him, but God called him to the diocesan priesthood. With characteristic energy John plunged into seminary studies and life. A friend remarked that John was happiest when he had two irons in the fire at the same time.

After his ordination in 1945, Father John J. O'Connor was catapulted into parish work, teaching school and counseling. Another call came from the Lord. In 1952, Father O'Connor became a chaplain in the United States Navy. He served active duty both in Korea and Vietnam. The following citation was read to Chaplain O'Connor after his ministry in Da Nang, Vietnam (August 1965).

It is my opinion that no single individual in this command contributed more to the morale of the individual Marine here in Vietnam than Father O'Connor who spent the majority of his time in the field with the men.

By the time of his retirement from the U.S. Navy, Chaplain O'Connor had been promoted to the rank of Rear Admiral.

In 1979, Father O'Connor heard from Cardinal Cooke, Head of the United States Catholic Military Ordinariate Headquarters. He said, "John, you will be ordained a bishop. You will work out of the

New York headquarters." With his broad smile, John Joseph said another, "Your will be done, Lord God." Unselfishly, he continued working for the spiritual and physical needs of others. He contributed greatly to the Bishops' outstanding pastoral, "The Challenge of Peace: God's Promise and Our Response."

In 1983, Bishop John O'Connor promptly gave further obedience when Pope John Paul II made him Bishop of Scranton, Pennsylvania. Though he was only in Scranton for eight months, he was greatly loved by the people. He was to be called upon again:

John Joseph, you have been reassigned.
You will become Archbishop of New York.

In 1984, Bishop O'Connor found himself repeating his Scranton Diocese operation but on a larger scale. New Yorkers received their new Archbishop with open hearts. The whole world suddenly discovered a dynamic leader whose challenges to goodness were delivered in a unique style. With reporters he was comfortable, with the elderly grateful, with politicians direct, with religious people supportive, with family loving, and with the young all-embracing.

God loves John Joseph O'Connor because John Joseph O'Connor loves everyone.

Pope John Paul II

If someone asked you, "Who is the most frequently quoted person in the twentieth century?" you could safely answer, "Pope John Paul II, Head of the Roman Catholic Church."

Carol Wotyla was born in Wadowice, Poland on May 18, 1920. His mother died when he was a very young child and his father saw that Carol attended school every day. Mr. Wotyla was proud of his son's achievements, not only in academic work but also in art, music, drama and athletics. Carol was a familiar figure on the ski slopes. He also traveled some weeks with a school theatrical company.

War fell upon the people of Poland. Carol finished university and worked in an industrial quarry. He joined the Polish army, defending his country from the intrusion of a Communist government. Carol felt strongly a desire to become a priest, but because of the Communists, he had to go underground to pursue his studies for priesthood. He was ordained in 1946, and became known as Father Carol Wotyla.

Father Wotyla was quickly known as an outstanding priest. He took care of his people. He taught university classes and continued to spend time on the ski slopes. Father Wotyla believed in the adage, "A healthy body, a healthy mind."

The authorities in the Polish church requested that Father Carol be made a bishop. A bishop's main job is to be a teacher in the Catholic Church. Carol was consecrated Archbishop of Krakow in 1964, and was put in charge of the large diocese. Even the Polish Communist government recognized his brilliance and strength in teaching and caring for his Catholic people.

In 1967, Pope Paul VI called Bishop Wotyla into the College of Cardinals and Poland proudly cheered its new Cardinal Carol Wotyla. Some years later Pope Paul VI died. The Cardinals throughout the world came to Rome to elect a new Pope. They prayed and discussed the qualities the Pope should have. They elected a warm, smiling, Italian man, Cardinal Albino Luciano, who chose the name John Paul I. After only one month Pope John Paul I died very suddenly. Again the Cardinals voted. On October 16, 1978, they elected Cardinal Carol Wotyla who selected the name John Paul II.

Pope John Paul II moved to Rome to lead the world's millions of Catholics in the ways of Christianity. His main concern was that Catholics keep true to the Gospel of Jesus and to the traditions of the Church. He urged Catholics, indeed peoples of all religions, not to give full reign to the instincts of self-interest, sex and power. He told young people not to be afraid of honest effort and honest work. With Christ's help, he said, and through prayer, you can answer His call, resist temptation and fads, and every form of mass manipulation.

In 1979, John Paul II visited the United States

and praised the American people's desire to be free, to preserve freedom, and their willingness to share this freedom with others. Pope John Paul II is concerned that all people in the world be free to have those things in life that are rightfully theirs; namely, food, shelter, clothing, honest work, a sense of dignity and pride in themselves, their families and their friends.

Perhaps the most meaningful statement John Paul II ever made was to young girls and boys everywhere. He said, "The most beautiful and stirring adventure that can happen to you is the personal meeting with Jesus, who is the only one who gives real meaning to our life."

Father Patrick Peyton

"Mary will come and pray with you to her Son Jesus who is with God His Father in Heaven. He cannot deny His Blessed Mother anything she asks." For forty years Father Patrick Peyton gave these loving words of assurance to people in almost every country in the world. In the movement known as the Family Rosary Crusade, Father Peyton urges families to pray the Rosary.

Patrick Peyton was born on January 9, 1909, in a three-room thatched cottage in County Mayo, Ireland. The youngest boy, he helped out at the farm with his brothers and sisters. Food was scarce but John and Mary Gillard Peyton saw that their nine children had plenty of love and warmth. Every night they prayed together the family rosary. The Blessed Mother smiled lovingly as she heard the young voices tell over and over again the story of her Son, Jesus.

As he grew older, Patrick heard the call of the Lord to be a priest. In 1928, Patrick and his brother Thomas went to the United States, and joined their sister Nellie in Scranton, Pennsylvania. His father's parting words to Patrick were, "Be faithful to Our Lord in America."

In 1929, Patrick and Tom entered the Holy Cross Fathers Seminary at Notre Dame, Indiana. Both young men studied hard. During his seminary days, Patrick became very ill with tuberculosis and the doctors feared for his life. Father Patrick prayed especially hard to the Blessed Mother and attributed his complete recovery to prayers, especially to the prayers of his sister Nellie and his mother. After his recovery, Patrick received special permission for ordination. Patrick Joseph and Thomas Francis Peyton were ordained Holy Cross priests on June 15, 1941.

It took Father Pat from June 15, 1941, the day he was ordained a priest, until January, 1942 to find the perfect way to express his profound gratitude for his recovery. "Then God struck like lightning," he says. "I was thinking of a thousand ways to say thanks and all of a sudden, the idea of the Family Rosary came to me. I knew that was the answer."

Father Peyton asked God and Mary to direct him in his future work. He discovered, by listening to God in his heart, that he should dedicate his life to prayer and the Family Rosary. He became a missionary to every family in America. Father Theodore Hesburgh, the future president of the University of Notre Dame, was the young seminarian who typed Father Peyton's first invitation to the families of America for the Family Rosary campaign. Father Hesburgh believed in Father Peyton. You perhaps have heard the expression "And a little child shall lead them." Helping Father Peyton with his crusade was Sister Magdalena and her high school students. They typed and addressed thousands of letters to pastors all over the United States to help begin the Family Rosary Crusade.

They loved to listen to his soft Irish brogue. Father Peyton thanked them for their work. When Father Peyton needed money for stamps, it was the school children who donated the money.

The Family Rosary Crusade began in small parishes and at school meetings. The idea spread like wildfire. Bishops, priests and sisters, brothers and lay people began to ask Father Peyton for his Rosary Crusade. On May 13, 1945, Father Peyton broadcast the story of the Rosary on national radio for the first time. Soon after, Father Peyton went to Los Angeles and had a Church Prayer meeting. Movie stars were invited to attend. Father Peyton told the story of his faith and family and of his remarkable recovery from lengthy illness. He described the power of the Rosary in his life. He asked the Hollywood stars to help in the crusade. Actors and actresses responded to his plea. Workers in his crusade included Bing Crosby, Grace Kelly, Irene Dunne, Pat O'Brien, Jimmy Durante and Ann Blythe. Business people like Conrad Hilton and J. Peter Grace gave generously to the cause of the Family Rosary and the Family Theater.

On February 13, 1947, the first production of Father Peyton's Family Theater appeared on television. In the years that followed, Gregory Peck, Jimmy Durante, Perry Como, Ethel Barrymore, Maureen O'Hara, Ricardo Montalban, and many other Hollywood stars appeared on Father Peyton's shows.

Family Rosary, Inc. and Family Theater, Inc. were both incorporated in 1947. They are now a part of Crusade for Family Prayer, Inc. which was incorporated in 1954. The phrase, "The family that prays together stays together," is attributed to Father Peyton and is officially recognized as a proverb.

Because of a loving commitment, energy and faith, Patrick Peyton, once a poor Irish farm boy, has traveled the world telling of the love which Jesus and Mary have for every man, woman and child.

Father Bruce Ritter

Bruce Ritter was born in Trenton, New Jersey on February 25, 1927. After graduating from high school, he joined the United States Navy. The U.S. Navy could never know that one of her loyal servicemen was listening to the Lord calling him to become a Franciscan priest. It was one of the things one didn't talk too readily about on the high seas.

He completed his naval service in 1946, and applied for admission to the Order of Friars Minor Conventual, popularly known as the Franciscans, in 1947. Father Ritter was ordained in 1956, and awarded a doctorate in medieval theology in Rome in 1958.

After returning to the United States, Father Ritter taught at St. Anthony-on-Hudson Seminary and Canevin High School. A sharp critical thinker, Father Ritter saw through many of the injustices in society. He challenged his students to study the causes of poverty and crime in big cities. Father Ritter was an on-target teacher.

Father Bruce was assigned to Manhattan College in the Bronx in 1963. This assignment would change his life. In 1968, at the urging of his students, he asked to live and work amongst the poor.

When permission was granted, Father Bruce moved into a housing project on Manhattan's

Lower East Side. Covenant House had its beginnings soon thereafter on one cold winter evening when six homeless children, four boys and two girls, knocked on his door. Father Ritter offered them shelter for the night, and the following day four more children arrived. Father Bruce's apartment was small, but he looked at the ten young children and suddenly realized the power he had to help them. He remembered the challenge his college students had issued to him. His very life as a follower of Christ and as a Franciscan priest challenged him. On this day, the seeds of his new work were planted.

In 1972, his ministry was chartered as Covenant House, and in 1977, he opened Under 21 in Times Square. The initial funding for Covenant House and Under 21 came from the Roman Catholic Archdiocese of New York, the Franciscans and the Charles E. Culpepper Foundation. Other money was begged by Father Ritter at eight or nine Masses every weekend at churches around the metropolitan area.

From its beginning in 1960, Father Bruce's work with children has been based on deep personal and community prayer. He offers safety from the street. He offers help to young people who steal, lie, cheat and run away from their homes. These children are hungry, confused and frightened. They are hurting children. One of Father Bruce's biggest works is to instruct teachers to educate their students in the subjects of civics and voting. He knows that once the crooked people in political offices are rooted out,

the chances of cleaning up the streets, ferreting out the porno racketeers and stopping the illegal drug traffic are great.

Father Bruce Ritter spends a lot of time talking to high school students. He even cancels other dates to make room for them. He hopes that some words he says will head off a student who might be thinking of leaving home. He feels that the high school students will do better things in the future to help people live happy lives.

Father Bruce has opened Covenant House, Under 21 and crisis centers in New York, Toronto, Houston, Boston and Guatemala. The centers offer health and legal advice. They provide opportunities for educational and vocational counseling. They give mother/child care to pregnant teenagers. The wonderful thing that the crisis centers have unearthed is the beauty of the young people. Once they respond to help they become even more beautiful.

Covenant House and Under 21 is an international, nonprofit agency dedicated to the care and shelter of homeless and runaway youth. With the help of wonderful men and women, Father Bruce Ritter does the work of Jesus who becomes for many lonely, frustrated teenagers the Way, the Truth and the Life.

Archbishop Oscar Romero

El Salvador has been called the "Tom Thumb" of America. The tiny country of over 5 million people is the land where a wonderful martyr of our modern day world was born, lived and died. His name is Archbishop Oscar Romero y Galdamez.

There is not too much to tell about Oscar Romero's life as a young boy. He was born in 1917, in Ciudad Barrios, a city on the border with Honduras. His father, Santos Romero, was a telegraph operator. Everybody knew that his mother, Guadalupe de Jesus, was a very kind and generous woman who was close to her family and to Jesus.

When Oscar was very young, he began his studies. He was bright and conscientious. He felt a call to priesthood and he entered the seminary in San Salvador. He was ordained a priest in 1942. The following year he was sent to Rome, Italy, for further studies.

Father Romero returned to El Salvador and ministered as a parish priest in Anamoros. He later took care of the people in the big Cathedral parish. Father Romero also did work as secretary at the meetings of bishops and priests. He was a quiet, diligent worker.

Father Romero was ordained a bishop in 1970. He worked with Archbishop Luis Chavez in San Salvador. Four years later Bishop Romero took

charge of the diocese of Santiago de Maria. The people he ministered to had good jobs and made good money. However, Father Romero did not fully realize that so many other people in El Salvador were very, very poor. He would soon learn this horrible truth.

In 1977, when Bishop Romero became Archbishop of San Salvador, his priests told him many stories about the *campesinos*, the people who worked on the land owned by the few rich families in the country. Archbishop Romero walked among the people and saw for himself the awful conditions in which they lived. He knew that Jesus loved the poor. His own heart was so moved to compassion that he told the wealthy families and the government leaders to help the oppressed people. He began to understand what the priests and sisters who worked with the poor were all about. He saw the love and peace of Jesus in their lives. He also saw them, as well as Salvadoran people, being murdered. They were trying to bring justice where unjust practices were keeping the poor in suffering and pain.

Archbishop Romero used letters, newspaper articles, the pulpit and the radio, to let the world know the sufferings of his people. This angered the government leaders, the wealthy and even some other bishops. Archbishop Romero said, "There can be no church unity if we ignore the world in which we live."

Archbishop Romero received threats against his life. He was frightened. He said that if he were killed his blood would be the seed of freedom. He wanted his people to be free. He truly loved as Jesus loved. He gave his people confidence, and spirit, and hope.

On March 24, 1980, as Archbishop Romero was celebrating Mass, he was assassinated. He was truly one with the martyred people of El Salvador.

Listen to what one priest who was a close friend of Archbishop Romero wrote about him:

"Together with thousands of Salvadorans I have seen Jesus. This time his name was Oscar Arnulfo Romero. His broken body is broken with the body of Jesus, his shed blood is shed with the blood of Jesus. And as with Jesus, so it is with Monsenor, he died for us that we might live in freedom and in love and justice for one another."

Babe Ruth

If he were alive, George Herman Ruth would smile for many reasons. One of them would be that the public praises him for becoming part of American folklore. For "Babe," as this well-loved character is best known, fame lay in the game of baseball and not in his name. However, history proves it is a bit of both. The name "Babe Ruth" is as well known as "Yankee baseball," and the game of baseball itself.

Babe was born on February 6, 1895, in Baltimore, Maryland. He lived in a tough neighborhood near the docks and learned all the street language and antics of the day. Babe went to sleep at night with the familiar smells and sounds from the busy saloon below his parents' apartment. This was the environment in which Babe grew up.

Because of his undisciplined nature, Babe's father registered him in St. Mary's Industrial School for Boys, which was run by the Xaverian Brothers. Babe became a Catholic while he was at St. Mary's and the Xaverian Brothers became his surrogate parents. He settled nicely into the school and boasted that those nine years at St. Mary's were the best of his life.

The Xaverian Brothers were men who really cared about the boys. They taught basic reading, writing and mathematics. Each boy was equipped for a job at an honest trade when he left school. More important than basic studies, the Brothers taught the boys how to live decently in society. Through their personal lives the Brothers proved that love of God and neighbor was a more important quest than desire for great riches. Under the Brothers' guidance Babe learned how to pray and received the sacraments on a regular basis.

Of all the Brothers, Brother Matthias, the prefect of discipline, had the greatest influence on Babe. Brother Matthias was the ideal father figure that Babe needed and took the young boy under his wing. All his life Babe would publicly state that Brother Matthias was the greatest man he'd ever known.

Babe's fondest memories of school centered on learning baseball. He started as a left-handed pitcher. He said, "I felt a strange relationship with the pitching mound. It was as if I had been born out there. Pitching just felt like the most natural thing in the world. Striking out batters was easy."

The rumblings of war could be heard throughout Europe in 1914. Babe was 18 years old, 6' 2" tall and weighed over 200 pounds. He was signed by the Baltimore Orioles as a left-handed pitcher, and his contract was immediately sold to the Boston Red Sox. Within five short years, Babe pitched in the World Series, winning three games and losing none. He set a World Series record of twenty-nine consecutive scoreless innings, a record which took baseball pitchers many years to break.

Babe was sold to the New York Yankees in 1920 for $125,000 and the rest is baseball history.

In 1920, the eyes of the world turned to the New York Yankees. No ball park anywhere had an empty seat when the Yankees came to play. Why? Babe Ruth gave performances that made baseball the most exciting spectator sport in the world. In 1921, he hit 59 home runs, batted in 170 RBI's and had a .378 average; in 1927, Babe hit 60 home runs, knocked in 164 RBI's and achieved a .356 average. Over the course of his illustrious career, Babe would hit 714 home runs, knock in 2,209 RBI's and maintain a .342 average. Babe Ruth, perhaps the greatest man ever to play the game of baseball, was elected as a charter member to Baseball's Hall of Fame in 1936. He died of cancer on August 16, 1948.

Thomas O'Connor, a parking lot attendant who saw Babe Ruth star in many games, had this to say about him.

"Babe Ruth always had a tender heart, especially for young children. As he stepped up to the bat, he would send a prayer heavenwards that the ball would be a lucky one, hit for a particular suffering child in a hospital somewhere in the country."

One can imagine the lifelong habit that Babe Ruth had acquired of speaking and listening to the Lord in prayer. During many hours of practice to perfect his pitching and batting skills, he was in God's presence. It was a habit begun in his early days and for which he owed another debt of gratitude to his much beloved Brother Matthias.

St. Elizabeth Ann Seton

One woman in American Catholic Church history embodies a variety of role models. Elizabeth Ann Bayley Seton is an inspiration for people who love life, family, friends and Church.

Elizabeth Ann was born on August 28, 1774, in New York. Her father, Dr. Richard Bayley, practiced medicine in the New York colony. When Elizabeth was three years old, her mother died and Dr. Bayley remarried. Elizabeth and her two sisters were joined by six more children. Psalm 23, "The Lord is My Shepherd," was a favorite Bayley family prayer.

There were difficult days when the American colonies won their independence. Cities had to be rebuilt. Rioting often occurred and diseases ran rampant. In New York, Elizabeth found herself terrified for her father's safety. At night Dr. Bayley spent long nights trying to save people's lives. He served the poor by opening the Staten Island Dispensary which gave medical help to the needy.

It was in her early romantic awakening period that Elizabeth Ann met young William Seton. He served as an accountant in his father's mercantile business. William and Elizabeth shared an interest in music. While Elizabeth accompanied him on the piano, Will played many tunes on his precious Stradivarius violin. Elizabeth Ann married her

"dearest treasure" on January 25, 1794. She was 19 years old.

Elizabeth was greatly loved by William's family. The young couple and their children enjoyed summer fun on the shores of the East River at the tip of Manhattan Island. When Will's mother died, he and Elizabeth took in six of his brothers and sisters. Elizabeth often prayed for patience.

Disaster soon fell upon Elizabeth. Her husband's business failed and William contracted tuberculosis. To help him get better Elizabeth took him to Italy. Unfortunately, William died in the home of his dear friends, the Filicchi family, in 1803.

It was because of the Filicchi family that the heartbroken Elizabeth became interested in the Catholic Church. She saw in the Italian family a fervent love for Jesus in Holy Communion. They fasted and did penance for their sins. Elizabeth loved prayer, a characteristic which her Episcopalian minister, Reverend Henry Hobart, had helped to nourish. Now, a deeper desire for the Lord stirred her soul. In 1805, Elizabeth returned to New York and took instructions to become a Catholic. Her minister and friends were upset. Catholics were not respected in New York. To meet financial expenses Elizabeth ran a small boarding school. She tutored her daughters Anna, Catherine and Rebecca, while Richard and William, her two sons, went to Georgetown. The boys' expenses were paid for by Antonio Filicchi.

Even though she had five children to raise, Elizabeth heard God calling her to become a sister.

She wanted to enter a convent in Montreal. Instead she traveled south to Baltimore, Maryland with her three girls. There she took over a small private school. In less than a year, four women joined Elizabeth. On June 21, 1809, the group set out for Emmettsburg, a country farm estate that would serve as their new home. There began the Sisters of Charity. They decided to become a new community of religious sisters with Elizabeth as their head. The new house had only four rooms for sixteen people. They slept on mattresses, carried in water, and washed their clothes in Tom's Creek. Everything was so different from what Elizabeth had been used to in her wealthy childhood home.

The little community was no sooner started when Anna became ill and died. It was a devastating blow and Mother Seton found it extremely difficult to cope with Anna's death. Only her faith and trust in God's love saw her through the ordeal.

The Sisters of Charity adopted the spirituality of Saint Vincent de Paul. Like Jesus and Dr. Bayley, St. Vincent had always placed the needs of the poor first in his life. Like him Elizabeth and the other sisters became models for women who wanted to love God in a special way. More women joined the small group and larger living quarters were built. Before long, the Sisters of Charity were caring for needs of people, poor and rich, all over the United States.

Elizabeth Seton died on January 4, 1821. She said she considered being brought into the Catholic Church the greatest blessing bestowed on her by God. She felt God's presence throughout her entire life.

In 1975 Elizabeth was canonized a saint in St. Peter's Church in Rome. She is indeed a universal role model for mothers, sisters, single women, and for everyone who loves God.

Bishop Fulton Sheen

Archbishop Fulton Sheen smiled as he read the little boy's message. "I hop you have a happy birthday. I hop that you will live long. I hop that one day you will be pop." It was the Archbishop's 84th birthday. He prided himself in caring little about living long and being Pope. He cared about service to the homeless and to the hungry. He saw Jesus in every stranger who was in need.

Peter Fulton Sheen was born in El Paso, Illinois on May 8, 1895. When Newton Sheen's hardware store burned down, he moved his wife, Delia, and his sons to a farm outside Peoria. Fulton liked school work much better than his farm work. He was a very bright student and did very well in his studies.

God gifted Fulton with a remarkable memory. The Lord also gave Fulton a vocation to priesthood. He answered the call and was ordained a Catholic priest in Peoria in 1919. Father Sheen was given a teaching assignment. He became a famous teacher. He told his students that teaching is one of the noblest vocations on earth.

In 1930, the Reverend Fulton Sheen began a radio talk show called the "Catholic Hour." For twenty years thousands of Catholic and non-Catholic families sat around their radios on Sunday nights listening to lively stories with lessons about life, living and God.

In 1951, Fulton Sheen was ordained a bishop in the Catholic Church. Bishop Sheen was delighted that he was born in the electronic age. The time was ripe, he said, to use TV as a means of communicating God's love to the American people. He began a TV series called "Life is Worth Living." Bishop Sheen won an Emmy Award in 1952 for the "Life is Worth Living" series.

One of Bishop Sheen's greatest joys was his job as national director of the Society of the Propagation of the Faith. Fulton Sheen showed he had a global spirituality. He was happy that the Good Lord had made him a beggar for His mission cause. He said that hunger was not just an economic problem but a moral and spiritual problem as well. Fulton Sheen spent sixteen years begging for money to help missionary brothers, sisters and priests feed hungry people in foreign countries.

Bishop Sheen also found time to be a prolific writer. Millions of people read and quoted from his column called "God Love You." Here are some of the Bishop's own words:

> I always prepare my work in the presence of the Blessed Sacrament.
> The most brilliant ideas come from meeting God face to face.
> A worker always works better when the Beloved is within Him.
> Divinity always seems to be where it is least expected.
> Jesus made Himself a ZERO. He humbled himself.

I am not afraid to meet God, not because
my love is so great but because God's love
is so great for me!
Think about your own time spent with God.
Do you talk? Or, do you mostly listen?

Bishop Fulton Sheen died on December 10,
1969.

Francis Cardinal Spellman

It was Christmas eve in the war-torn country of Korea. American soldiers stationed there awaited the arrival of Cardinal Francis Spellman who would say a special Midnight Mass for them. The plane landed safely. Cardinal Spellman stepped forward. He was greeted by Army chaplain Father William Moran and military leaders. "Bill," he whispered to Chaplain Moran, "have you the cigarettes and medals for the men?" Receiving a nod, the Cardinal began to shake hands with the servicemen who had eagerly lined up to meet him. Chaplain Moran stood on the other side passing over medals. Cardinal Spellman gave the gifts to each person along with messages of hope.

May 4, 1889, was the birthdate of Francis Joseph Spellman. Willie and Nellie Spellman gave their five children a happy home in the little town of Whitman, Massachusetts. The children had regular household chores. Francis delivered papers, tended his father's store, helped with the haying, rode horses. Francis attended the local public school. He played hockey and was first baseman on Whitman High School's baseball team. Francis won several prizes for outstanding essays. At graduation he won scholarships to Notre Dame and Fordham. He chose Fordham.

College days were memorable for Francis. He

did well in his studies and played baseball and tennis. He joined the Dramatic Society and acted in several Shakespearean plays. Essays and editorials written by Francis Spellman appeared in the college newspaper. On his Commencement Day in 1911, Francis told his parents that he wanted to be a priest. Giving him their blessings, Willie and Nellie watched their son sail aboard the Cunard RMS Franconia to the North American College in Rome.

Francis Spellman was ordained a priest on May 14, 1916. He said his first Mass at the tomb of St. Peter. His first assignments sent him as chaplain to a home for the aged in Boston, to a church in Roxbury, the office of the Boston Catholic newspaper, the Chancery office and then to an office in Rome. While in Rome he took charge of building playgrounds for children. He fell in love with Rome and on February 8, 1929, Father Spellman wrote, "These are wonderful days to be alive and still more wonderful to be alive and in Rome." Father Spellman brought a great enthusiasm to his life as a priest. He became a friend to poor and rich alike. He formed a warm friendship with Cardinal Pacelli, who later became Pope Pius XII.

Father Spellman's talents, generosity, intelligence and deep faith in God singled him out as a capable leader. He was made a bishop in 1932, by Cardinal Pacelli, and was sent to work in Boston. In 1939, he became Archbishop of New York. As Archbishop, Francis Spellman had many big jobs as pastor of several million people. He made changes in education to help children and people.

He provided education for children from poor black and Spanish families, including non-Catholics. He helped hospitals and charities, Catholic Relief Services and universities. He wrote nine books and helped edit the *New Catholic Encyclopedia*. He also wrote poetry and fiction. Later, he opened a closed circuit television station for Catholic schools. Archbishop Spellman, popular with leaders of the nation and the Church, was consecrated a Cardinal on February 21, 1946.

One of Cardinal Spellman's greatest joys was heading the Military Ordinariate where he could pray for and visit the servicemen and women all over the world. He wrote a fervent prayer:

And if it be
My blood should mingle reverently with Christ's,
His Son's, in this my final missioning,
Shall I not whisper with my dying breath—-
Lord, it is sweet to die—as it were good
to live, to strive—for these United States.

Cardinal Spellman died on December 2, 1967.

From his earliest years Francis Spellman used the energy and talents God had given him to live his life to its fullest. Although always very active, he took time each day to praise and thank God for everything. Francis Spellman was truly an outstanding Catholic.

Sister Eileen Storey

Eileen Storey was born on April 7, 1925. The proverb that she best remembers from her Irish parents' storehouse of maxims is "The Best Things in Life Are Free." For Eileen that has meant discovering that life is joyous because of the wonderful people, places and things that the good Lord has freely placed on this earth. Freely given, these gifts were freely received by the grateful Eileen.

While a child Eileen traveled from her birthplace in Ireland to the United States. Eileen and her brother Tom settled into a new way of life. They had twelve years of Catholic school training. Mr. Storey taught his children to be perfectionists. After graduation God called Eileen to be a Sister of Charity. She smiles as she remembers thinking that she had, at that time, all the answers to life's big questions.

Eileen succeeded well in all her studies. Imagine seeing your name in print with five college degrees written after it! After her profession, Eileen's congregation sent her to teach French and English to high school students. It wasn't long before many students considered Sister Eileen their most popular teacher. She later spent ten years in the Bahamas, at Xavier College and Her Majesty's Prison!

In 1968, Eileen was called back to the United

States and was assigned the job of Directress of Novices. This meant she had to train other women to become sisters.

The Lord proposed another great plan to Sister Eileen. In her usual manner, she said, "All right, Lord. Whatever You wish, I will do it." God knew that Eileen had a special love for all people, especially for those men, women, boys, and girls, who had strong desires to know God through a special life of prayer. These people needed a guide to help them. God called Sister Eileen to be that guide. In 1971, she began to set up houses where people could pray and worship God.

Sister Eileen's warm love, twinkling sense of humor, and obvious sense of the presence of God soon attracted many people to the House of Prayer Movement. In these houses God is loved and praised. The lonely, hungry, sick, homeless, prisoners, abandoned, hurting and the orphans are prayed for. Government and church leaders are prayed for. People in Houses of Prayer frequently are inspired to go out and help change the structures in society that make other people depressed and sad. Sister Eileen herself runs a soup kitchen for hungry city people.

A personal achievement for Sister Eileen was spending a year in Japan and India. She visited ashrams, talked to people, and prayed in silent meditation. She learned techniques that make use of the Jesus prayer, breathing and Hatha Yoga. Sister Eileen brought back to the United States something Americans always had but didn't make much use of: the richness of meditation and contemplation.

Eileen Storey, an outstanding, much loved woman, is truly an outstanding Catholic. She teaches others to pray. She feeds the hungry. She understands what it means to be free to love God and others with her whole heart and soul. She understands what her lovely Irish parents meant when they would remind their children that the best things in life are free.

What are some of the best things that you enjoy in God's world that are free?

Mother Teresa

In 1984, the Winter Olympics were held in Sarajevo, Yugoslavia. The eyes of the world turned toward that European country whose mountain slopes glistened with pure white snow. It was in that same country that God brought to life a baby girl who has become in the eyes of the world the famous Mother Teresa of Calcutta.

Agnes Gonxha Bojaxhiu was born in Skopje, Yugoslavia on August 27, 1910. Agnes walked the mountain roads of Skopje to a government school with her brother and sister. These were happy, carefree days. She was 13 years old when she heard God speak to her. He asked if she would take care of the poor when she grew up. She said in her heart, "Here I am, Lord." When Agnes was 18 years old, she joined the Sisters of Loretto in Dublin, Ireland. Sister Teresa took her first vows in 1928, and her final vows in 1937. After training to be a missionary in Ireland and India, Sister Teresa went to St. Mary's High School in Calcutta where she taught girls. Sister Teresa loved teaching, and the bright and loving Indian girls loved her in return.

In 1946, God again called Sister Teresa. This time she was asked to leave the Loretto Sisters and to start a new group of sisters who would teach the poor street children. Again Teresa said, "Here I am, Lord." It was not easy to leave the Sisters of Loretto whom she loved. However, cries of the poor children were so loud that Sister Teresa heard not the tears in her own heart.

For the first time the poor little children of Calcutta had a chance to learn in school. How they enjoyed reciting their A B C's! When Sister Teresa saw that the children needed health care, too, she took classes in a medical school. Prepared to enter the people's homes, Sister Teresa saw many children and adults who were sick and dying. So much work had to be done for them. Sister Teresa soon found she had more than school children to care for. God helped her out by sending young, generous women to help teach the children and care for the sick and dying. These women started a religious community with Sister Teresa as their head sister.

In 1950, the Holy Father gave the Sisters of the Missionaries of Charity official status in the Church. Sister Teresa became known as Mother Teresa.

Mother Teresa and the sisters are tireless in their work for the poor. They teach poor children. They nurse the sick. They prepare the dying for a happy death. They believe that everybody, especially the poor, is worthy of love and care because each is made in God's image. Their gift of love is repaid by a happiness that only God can give.

Mother Teresa knows that God doesn't call everyone to be a missionary sister, brother or priest. She teaches the Gospel message of Jesus which says to care for the sick, feed the hungry, clothe the naked, shelter the homeless, visit the imprisoned and take strangers into your homes. The boys and girls, men and women, who hear and follow this teaching of Jesus are also outstanding Christians.

Mother Teresa of Calcutta has become famous all over the world. The Missionaries of Charity have expanded their ministry throughout India, Venezuela, Australia, England, Jordan, Italy and some of the larger cities in America such as Chicago and New York.

Mother Teresa has received many awards for her work with the poor. In 1971, she received both the Pope John XXIII Peace Prize and the Joseph P. Kennedy Jr. International Award. In 1979, Mother Teresa received the Nobel Peace Prize.

What has been the secret of Mother Teresa's great success? It has been her faith. She believes faith is a gift of God. Without it there would be no life. A Catholic person's work, to be fruitful, has to be built on faith and belief in God's graces which help us in all our works for others.

Maisie Ward

Imagine yourself walking out in a nearby wooded path with your father and his close friend, Alfred Lord Tennyson, the Poet Laureate of England. At your birth he had announced that you looked like King Henry the Eighth! Or picture yourself one rainy day curled up lazily in a big chair. You have a book by your favorite author, Jane Austen, and you are lost in the imaginary tale written by this great English writer. Perhaps another day you might find yourself in a bright study in your own home being tutored in reading and writing because you were not attending public school. All around you is conversation that is literary, artistic, philosophical, witty, and sacredly religious. You enjoy every moment of your childhood. Such was the childhood of Maisie Ward Sheed!

Maisie Ward was born on January 4, 1889, on the Isle of Wight, off the southern coast of England. Her father's family practically owned the whole town of Cowes. Maisie Ward's early childhood prepared her for a life filled with interesting literary and religious people. When her family moved to Surrey, Maisie attended private school. Her specialties were Latin and Scripture.

In April of 1926, Maisie married a brilliant Australian gentleman, Frank Sheed. Because of their great love of the Catholic Church, they established a publishing house for Catholic writers in October of that same year. It spread through England, Australia and the United States. Sheed and Ward Publishing Co. quickly became famous and well respected in the publishing world.

Maisie and Frank used well their tremendous gifts of writing and public speaking. They loved Jesus and His Gospel message so much that they used their talents to spread that good news. They encouraged other gifted people to join them in that work. G.K. Chesterton, Hillaire Belloc, Dorothy Day, Caryll Houselander and Christopher Dawson are some famous Catholic writers whose works were published by Maisie and Frank. Maisie's own books include *Gilbert Keith Chesterton, Young Mr. Newman, The Splendor of the Rosary, The Saints of Pictures* and *Be Not Solicitous.*

Maisie Ward's extraordinary gifts of writing and publishing did not distract her from seeing the needs of the poor in her English society. In 1955, she co-founded the Catholic Housing Aid Society, which helped homeless people by lending them money for building materials. She followed carefully the works of Dorothy Day and Baroness Catherine Von Hueck. These great women worked unselfishly for the poor. They established shelters and homes for the hungry and homeless. Sheed and Ward would publish books by these two great women.

Rosemary and Wilfred Sheed, Maisie's two children, remember their parents Maisie and Frank, as unique characters in the sense that they did what they did, never expected it all to last, and had fun. Maisie once wrote that she was grateful for her husband's laughter and for her children's, too. Both children truly mourned their mother, Maisie, who died on January 28, 1975. Frank wrote his fond memories of her in a lovely book called *One Particular Heart*.

What made Maisie Ward perhaps the most outstanding Catholic woman of the twentieth century? Her simple faith in God's presence and love. Her fruitful use of the tremendous talents God had given her. Her faithfulness to her husband Frank, her family and the homeless. Her beautiful sense of humor. Maisie Ward lived well the Scripture passage, "Consider the lilies of the field." She will long be remembered as a bright, colorful flower in the Lord's garden of witnessing Catholics.

Outstanding
CHILDREN'S BOOKS

Available from your local dealer or religious book store.

_____America's leading First Communion Books_____

No. 1525 **The Marian Children's Mass Book**

No. 1580 **First Steps to Jesus**

- Large choice of beautiful, durable bindings.
- Available for boys and girls in wallets, purses or Presentation Sets.

_____New and Recent Best Sellers_____

No. 1412 **The Life of Jesus**
No. 1515 **Biographies: God at Their Sides**
No. 1520 **The New Testament**
No. 1560 **First Penance**
No. 1550 **First Holy Communion**
No. 1700 **Mass Prayers for Children**
No. 1701 **Bible Prayers for Children**
No. 1703 **The New Testament for Children**
No. 1704 **The Life of Jesus**
No. 1708 **The Rosary for Children**
No. 1709 **The Ten Commandments for Children**
No. 1710 **The Way of the Cross for Children**
No. 1713 **The Beatitudes for Children**
No. 1716 **My First Mass Book**
No. 1717 **The Sacraments for Children**
No. 1400 **My First Bible**
No. 1400S **Mi Primera Biblia**
No. 1407 **My First Prayer Book**
No. 1408 **My First Book of Saints**
No. 1409 **The Story of Mary**
No. 1519 **The Catholic Children's Bible**